STEP-BY-STEP
MICROWAVE
COOKBOOK

STEP-BY-STEP
MICROWAVE
COOKBOOK

Cecilia Norman

BARRON'S

Woodbury, N.Y. • London • Toronto • Sydney

Acknowledgments

The author would like especially to thank her husband, Laurie, for all his support; Jenny Pouncett, who typed the manuscript, and Claudette McIntosh, for all her help with the preparation of recipes for this book.

The Publishers would also like to thank Corning, the manufacturers of Pyrex, for supplying items from their ranges of cookware for use in the photographs and line drawings.

Line drawings by John Woodcock.

First U.S. edition published 1985 by
Barron's Educational Series, Inc.

©1983 by Cecilia Norman and
the National Magazine Company Limited,
London, England

All inquiries should be addressed to:

Barron's Educational Series, Inc.
113 Crossways Park Drive
Woodbury, New York 11797

International Standard Book No. 0-8120-3562-3
Library of Congress Catalog Card No. 84-24377

Library of Congress Cataloging in Publication Data

Norman, Cecilia.
  The step-by-step microwave cookbook.

  Previously published as: The good housekeeping step-
by-step microwave cookbook. 1983.
  Includes index.
  1. Microwave cookery. I. Title.
TX832.N664 1985   641.5'882   84-24377
ISBN 0-8120-3562-3

PRINTED IN ITALY

5 6 7 8 9   9 8 7 6 5 4 3 2 1

Contents

Preface

The purpose of this special microwave cook book is to explain how to get the best results from your microwave oven, using step-by-step instructions on the various techniques. You will find all the information you need to understand how the microwave oven works and its effects on ingredients. It tells you which types of containers are suitable and which are not, which types of foods cook well in a microwave and which are best suited to conventional methods. All the basic techniques are explained in clear illustrations, and there is advice on how to adjust the cooking times on your own microwave oven so that the recipes will work well for you.

Each recipe section has an introduction giving all the information you need to produce excellent results. Step-by-step instructions take you through the simplest and most complicated recipes. If you are not familiar with microwave cooking I suggest you read all the introductions carefully and study the various techniques. Even if you are an experienced microwave cook, you may find a few extra tips that you did not know before.

Cecilia Norman

THE MICROWAVE COOKING SCHOOL
London, England

Introduction

People have odd ideas about microwave ovens. Some suppose them to be miraculous magic boxes, others wonder what on earth persuades people to pay upwards of $300 to cook a baked potato in 5 minutes. In fact, the microwave oven has many, many attributes and, in its own way, is more versatile than a freezer.

You may not have wanted a freezer originally but if you now have one you would not part with it. You will feel the same way about your microwave oven. You may even prefer to buy a microwave oven before you own a freezer.

The microwave oven is perhaps the most useful cooking appliance so far developed, because it fits perfectly with modern lifestyles and changing eating patterns. It is equally useful for the family or single person. It can defrost, reheat or carry out prime cooking, taking the place of both the stovetop and conventional oven for a high proportion of their cooking tasks. It goes hand-in-hand with the freezer, enabling you to store and reheat in the serving portions required, eliminating waste and offering a choice of dishes almost to order. Combined with the refrigerator, which can store food for short periods, it enables you to prepare food ahead, to be reheated quickly, safely and efficiently. The disabled and blind find it much easier to operate than a conventional stove.

The first obvious advantage of the microwave oven is the speed with which it can produce meals: it takes only a quarter to one-fifth of normal cooking times. And because microwave cooking is so quick, using the same amount of electricity as one conventional burner or element, there are savings in fuel consumption. Here are a few examples of the enormous savings in cooking time:

	Average time in minutes	
	Conventional	Microwave
Baked potato	60	5
Casserole	120	45
Fish (1 lb/450 g)	10	4
Lamb chops (2)	12	5
Roast chicken (3½ lb/1.5 kg)	90	25

The microwave oven also considerably cuts preparation and cleaning-up time, eliminating the worst washing-up chores.

Used in conjunction with a conventional stove, a microwave oven reduces the overall cooking time. Cook some component parts of a dish by microwave and some conventionally. For instance, a special roast-beef dinner can be hastened by par-cooking the potatoes and par-cooking the meat, and then browning them in a conventional oven just before you plan to serve the meal. You can then make a meringue pie or pudding in the microwave oven for dessert.

Use your microwave oven in conjunction with the freezer to store, thaw and reheat a greater selection of home-cooked or commercially prepared dishes. Garden produce can be blanched, or vegetables can be cooked and then stored in the freezer for subsequent reheating.

The microwave oven cooks in its own right too. Scrambled eggs are easy, fish dishes are fabulous and poultry cooks superbly. Vegetables retain their color and have a marvelous crisp texture. Jams can be made in small quantities just when you feel like using up an odd amount of fruit, and the microwave oven is excellent for sauces and candies. It cooks pasta and rice well, and although there is no significant saving in time over conventional methods, these foods are much easier to cook in the microwave oven as the cooking can be done in the dish in which the food will be served.

The microwave oven reheats perfectly without fear of spoiling or drying the food. Reheating times depend on the shape and density of the food and also the starting temperature—a pre-cooked frozen meal will take longer to reach eating temperature than a meal stored in the refrigerator. But generally speaking, a room temperature meal can be reheated in 2–3 minutes.

Quick Tips for the Microwave User

There are many small tasks that the microwave oven can be used for, either before you start cooking by microwave or when using conventional methods. Try using it for softening butter, melting chocolate, dissolving gelatine and heating small quantities of liquid.

Cake making

Melt chocolate for cakes and icings. If the butter is too firm to cream with the sugar, you can soften it by putting it in the microwave oven for a few seconds; do not melt it.

Jam making

Open the sugar carton and put the entire package in the microwave oven. The warm sugar will then dissolve more quickly when it is stirred into the fruit.

Flowers

Dry flowers in the microwave oven and bring back the perfume to a pot-pourri.

Mayonnaise

Take the chill off the vinegar and oil before making mayonnaise by microwaving on low for a few seconds.

Nuts

A lovely flavor is imparted to shelled nuts when they are microwaved on low until they just turn light brown inside. You will have to cut one or two in half to test for this.

Sauces

Heat milk for making white sauces or custards in the microwave on low for a few seconds.

Vegetables

If you want to lightly thaw frozen vegetables before adding them to stews, slash the packet first on top and microwave them for just a few seconds on low.

What are Microwaves?

Microwaves come into the same category as radio and television waves, sunlight, radar systems used in traffic control and infra-red fires. These waves are all known as non-ionizing rays, which means that they do not build up in the body and are therefore not dangerous. (Ionizing rays, on the other hand, do build up in the body. These include X-rays, gamma rays and cosmic rays, which are all short waves.) Microwaves travel in straight lines and are reflected by all types of metal.

There are few inner workings to a microwave oven. The main component is the magnetron, whose job it is to convert electricity into microwave energy. When you switch on, the magnetron starts to manufacture its microwaves and these invisibly enter the oven cavity and pass through the food. Every microwave oven is lined with metal, even though this may be covered by plastic or paint. So every time the microwaves reach the sides, top or bottom of the oven, they are reflected back again. They pass through the food at a rate of 2450 billion times a second, agitating the molecules in the food; these rub together causing friction, and it is the friction which heats the food. You could compare this to the warmth resulting from rubbing your hands together in cold weather. The more friction that occurs, the more cooking takes place.

When the oven is switched off or the door is opened, the microwaves disappear, but the food continues cooking until the heat inside the food diminishes.

The microwaves pass freely through glass, plastic, paper and other non-metallic materials and they are utilized by the food. Although the oven door is transparent, it is lined with perforated metal. The perforations are too tiny to allow the microwaves to pass through, ensuring that they are kept within the cooking cavity.

How microwaves work

Electric energy is converted to microwaves which are reflected by the oven's metals walls and pass straight through any non-metallic substances.

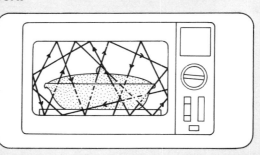

Microwaves, which are attracted to food, penetrate to a depth of about $1\frac{1}{2}$ inches (4 cm). The center of the food is cooked by conduction of heat generated in the outer layer.

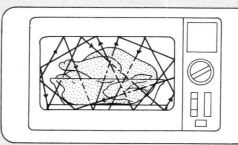

Microwave Ovens and Safety

There are two kinds of microwave oven—commercial and domestic. Very large powerful ovens have to be fitted with a special electric outlet but domestic models, which do not exceed 1.5 kw input (approximately 700 watts output), may be wired to a normal three-prong grounded plug.

Regarding safety, before leaving the factory, all microwave ovens are subjected to stringent tests and are required to satisfy the specific safety requirements.

When upacking your new oven check the doors are properly aligned and if in doubt ask for an engineer to check it over. Do not purchase a second-hand oven unless it has been approved by a microwave engineer. It may well be in first-class condition, but it is wise to have this confirmed as a new magnetron can be costly.

How Food Cooks in a Microwave Oven

In a microwave oven, all surfaces of the food are heated simultaneously to a depth of approximately $1\frac{1}{2}$ inches (4 cm). The microwave friction causes the heat and this then spreads by conduction. Because of the pattern of microwaves in the oven, the middle of any food receives mostly waves bounced off the top of the oven cavity. Consequently the food in the middle tends to cook more by conduction, while the sides are attacked by microwaves from all directions. This means that foods that can be, should be stirred or turned so that the middle has its turn at the edge of the container.

The air in a microwave cabinet is not heated; it remains at room temperature while only the food gets hot. So it is not possible to have a crisp outside and a soft inside to food. As the food cooks, moisture is drawn to the outside and the coolness of the cavity meets the hot food so that the surface remains soft and sometimes damp. Very little browning occurs. So, for example, a baked loaf will never have a crisp, brown crust and a piece of meat may be overcooked on the outside and yet the surface will not brown. You cannot make nicely browned pie crusts in the microwave oven, and meringues are hardly satisfactory.

There is a limit to the amount of food you can put in the microwave oven at any one time, so that the larger capacity of a conventional oven will sometimes produce better results than the speed of microwave cookery. For instance, a number of baking potatoes spaced out in the conventional oven would take about an hour to cook; only half a dozen can be cooked at a time in the microwave oven, although in approximately one-quarter of the time. So if you are cooking more than 24 potatoes at once, it is better to use the conventional oven.

Making sauces
When cooking on a conventional stovetop the lower surface of the pan becomes heated first, so that food particles may burn unless stirred. In the microwave oven there is no direct contact between the dish and the heat, so that surface burning cannot occur. Stirring is still necessary for even cooking, but less frequently. As a result, it is easier to make good sauces by microwave than by conventional stovetop cooking.

Frying
Deep frying is not possible in the microwave oven because of the lack of control of temperature, but onions and similar items can be browned well in a small amount of fat. Special browning dishes or plates are obtainable as optional extras. These are useful for searing and browning. Choose a browning dish which has a lid when you are going to start a dish by browning, for example chicken pieces or meat, and then finish by adding a sauce. Use the lid to keep in the moisture and the heat and prevent any splattering.

Boiling, poaching and steaming
Milk will boil over in the microwave oven just as it does on the stove, but if the LOW setting is used, there is less chance of this happening. On LOW you can also simmer and poach. For poaching, simmering or boiling three-quarters cover with plastic wrap and stir through the gap. Cooking starchy foods like potatoes or rice is much easier as the water will not bubble up and force off the lid as it often does on a stove. Steaming in the microwave oven is easy; no extra water is required, you just cover the dish with a lid or plastic wrap and the food cooks in its own moisture. You should steam with a loose cover of plastic wrap and a corner folded back so that the odd puff of steam can make its escape.

Broiling
A simple microwave oven is not suitable for broiling but there are a number of ovens on the market with grills and hot air devices for browning and searing, and browning dishes which help sear and brown the food. A microwave oven fitted with a grill is, of course, more difficult to clean. But if searing only is needed, (which

would be the equivalent of cooking in a frying pan), use a browning dish. Or cook the food by microwave and finish by browning under a broiler.

Baking

Microwaves can be used for making cakes, but they will not brown. This does not matter if dark ingredients such as chocolate or molasses are used or if the surface of the cake is to be covered with icing. Making pastry is not successful. Microwaves are attracted to fat and sugar, so that the interior of the pastry is inclined to scorch while the outside layer remains unaffected by the heat.

Browning and coating

Although the microwave oven doesn't sear, if ingredients would normally change color during cooking, such as syrups, they will do the same in the microwave oven. Nuts will roast and become brown inside and honey in a recipe is a particularly good browning ingredient. Where dark ingredients are used the food will achieve a deeper hue: use dark brown sugar, molasses, rich beef stock cubes, tomato purée, soy sauce, red wine, chocolate, cocoa and coffee essence to darken otherwise light foods.

Coatings can often improve the appearance of microwave-cooked food. Cakes can be iced or piped decoratively with whipped cream. Savory dishes can be covered in browned crumbs; these are even better if turmeric or paprika is included when melting the butter. There are also a number of commercial browning agents for use with the microwave oven.

Once you have discovered how easy it is to cook by microwave, you will become accustomed to the differences in color. You will find that the improvement in the texture and taste of many of the foods, plus the convenience and speed of cooking, will outweigh any resistance you may have to its appearance.

Microwave Cooking Techniques

All foods completely enclosed in a skin must be pricked or scored, cut or shelled before cooking. Otherwise the water molecules inside, which turn to steam, will burst and cause splattering.

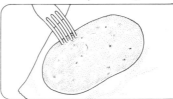

Microwaves are also attracted to fat, to water and to bones. Ingredients with a high fat content, such as cheese and egg yolks, overcook rapidly causing separation, curdling and toughening. Microwave these ingredients for a short time only or on a LOW setting.

Microwaves first cook around the outside of the food, unless it is so large that it covers the entire shelf. All ovens have a slightly uneven cooking pattern, with what are known as "hot spots." For even cooking, food must therefore be stirred or somehow repositioned during cooking. To test your oven for hot spots, arrange nine similar cups or glasses each containing the same amount of water at the same temperature on the oven shelf. Microwave on HIGH and those that boil first indicate the positions of the hot spots. If there is one particular place, either avoid putting the food in this part or make sure that you stir or turn.

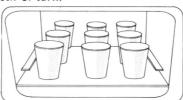

Foods that cannot be stirred because it would spoil the arrangement, and which similarly cannot be repositioned or turned over, can be evenly cooked by turning the dish. This is usually necessary even when the oven is fitted with a turntable. The recommended number of turns is given in the individual recipes.

Positioning and repositioning

Place thinner parts of food portions in the center and thicker parts around the outside of the dish. When several portions are being cooked in one dish and they are of similar size, they should be arranged in a single layer and repositioned during cooking so that those in the middle, receiving less microwaves, can change places with those on the outside, which will be receiving more.

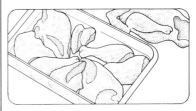

Turning over

Single items thicker than 2½ inches (6 cm) will cook more evenly if they are turned over once during cooking, because the microwave signal is stronger toward the upper part of the oven. This is particularly important when the food is not covered. When turning food over, reposition so that the outside parts are placed in the center of the dish.

Stirring and whisking

Stirring is necessary in exactly the same way as it is when cooking conventionally. Stir from the outside toward the center so that all the food is equally mixed. Whisking ensures even mixing to prevent lumpy sauces. It is specially important when the sauce contains critical ingredients such as eggs.

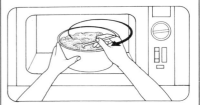

Covering with a lid or plastic wrap

Always cover food if a moist, even heat is required, so that the steam is trapped. The food then cooks by steam as well as by microwave.

Covering is particularly important to prevent evaporation when only a small amount of liquid is used. Use a lid or plastic wrap if stirring is necessary.

When the food is fairly liquid, three-quarters covering is often sufficient; tightly cover, then pull back one corner of the plastic wrap. You can then insert the spoon to stir through the gap. Use plastic wrap for complete covering only when the food is being reheated or cooked for a very short time, or if the food is being microwaved on LOW. When food is microwaved on HIGH or lengthy cooking periods are necessary, the plastic wrap must be vented. When removing plastic wrap peel it from the side furthest away from you so that the steam is directed away from your face.

Covering with paper
Use wax paper or non-stick paper for covering to prevent food from becoming soggy or if a consider-able amount of repositioning or turning is necessary. The paper may blow about in the microwave oven if it is fitted with a fan, so secure it with a wooden toothpick or lightly tuck the ends of the paper

underneath the dish. The latter method is only suitable for short time cooking as paper underneath dishes can catch fire. When covering for long periods, split open a roasting bag and tuck it completely underneath the dish.

When thawing or cooking food where heating will cause surface moisture, or when you wish to absorb any splattering of fat, use absorbent kitchen paper.

Shielding
To prevent parts of unstirrable foods from becoming over-cooked, cover vulnerable areas with small smooth pieces of foil pressed close to the food. Secure it with toothpicks, if there is any possibility of it's being blown off. Foil must not touch the interior lining of the oven or it will damage the magnetron. If preferred, overwrap with plastic wrap.

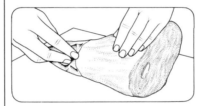

Standing time
When food is removed from the microwave oven a standing time is often allowed so that any uneven heat can equalize itself. This is part of the cooking process and should not be omitted. If a standing time is specified in the recipe, cover the food with a tent of foil when it is removed from the oven and allow the standing time indicated in the recipe. This is usually equal to the cooking time but not always.

Use of temperature probe and humidity detectors
A special microwave thermometer can be left in meat and poultry during cooking. Ordinary meat thermometers are not suitable and must not be used. A microwave meat thermometer is not usually suitable for use in syrups and jams, as the maximum reading is not high enough for boiling sugar.

A special microwave cooking thermometer is a probe which plugs into a socket inside the microwave oven. To use it, insert it into the thickest part of the meat or the center of a pudding. The maximum internal temperature for perfect cooking is then pre-set on the control panel of the microwave oven and the microwaves are shut off automatically when the food is ready. This method of testing is not always accurate since, if the probe is pushed into a fatty part of the food, the reading may not be correct. Microwave temperature probes are also inclined to be inaccurate when used in thin pieces of food.

Some ovens have a humidity detector which determines when the food is cooked. To use this the food must be completely covered with plastic wrap; the detector then picks up the first puff of steam emitted through the plastic wrap and calculates how long the food will require. These are excellent provided instructions are followed carefully and the quantities recommended are used, but these too occasionally allow some overcooking.

If you are using a thermometer or probe to determine when the food is cooked, follow the chart below.

Baby food	95°F (35°C)
Beverages	160°F (70°C)
Meat	
Beef	120–160°F (50–70°C)
Casseroles	150°F (65°C)
Lamb	175–180°F (80–85°C)
Pork	175–180°F (80–85°C)
Veal	175°F (80°C)
Soups	160°F (70°C)
Vegetable	
Casseroles	150°F (65°C)

Stacking
Meals on plates can be stacked with up to three plates, one above the other. There must be an air space between each plate and microwave stacking rings are ideal for this purpose. The top plate must be covered. It makes no different to the heating if the others are also covered. Mix the foods vertically so that the meat and various vegetables alternate throughout the stack.

Containers for Microwave Cooking

Cooking times

Cooking time in the microwave oven is in direct relation to the amount of food being cooked. A small quantity will cook much faster than a large, though it is not always necessary to double the amount of cooking time when doubling the quantity; there is a saving of time overall when larger amounts are being cooked. If one quantity or one item takes 1 minute, two quantities or two items which are similar in size will take only 1¾ minutes. As a rough guide increase the time by about half when the recipe is being doubled.

The cooking time given in recipes is always the lowest reasonable time, to ensure that you do not overcook. When timing always take into account any further instructions, such as "cook until tender" or "until thickened." Under-cooked food can be rectified, burnt food cannot.

Size of food portions

Small even-shaped portions will cook more successfully than large or uneven pieces. This is because the microwave signal penetrates to a depth of 1–1½ inches (2.5–4 cm), but after this the signal becomes weaker and cooking continues by conduction.

Starting temperatures

The colder the food, the longer the cooking time will be. The food temperature varies from refrigerator to refrigerator and likewise with the freezer. Non-frozen foods should be at room temperature, otherwise cooking times will be affected.

The one material which cannot be used in a microwave oven is metal. So ordinary saucepans and iron casseroles, or any container with a metallic trim of any description, are out. Otherwise you can choose from a wide range of ceramic, glass, wood, paper and plastic materials to suit your purpose. The shape of the container also affects the cooking speed.

Foods which are going to reach a very high temperature, such as those with a high sugar or fat content, must be cooked in dishes which can withstand these temperatures. Ovenglass is always a good choice, but some specialist microwave cooking ware can also be used. Re-usable plastics are extremely useful provided the food is not going to become too hot, and wood and straw can also be used in certain circumstances. A list of useful containers and the best way to use them is given in the chart on pages 13 to 15.

Browning dishes

Microwave browning dishes, such as those produced by Corning, are white in color but underneath you may notice a gray sheen. This is a special coating which attracts the microwaves. When the dish or plate is put into the microwave oven empty and heated for a few minutes, the surface becomes as hot as a frying pan. Unfortunately these browning dishes do not hold the heat for long and, once food is added, the browning capability diminishes fairly rapidly. The browning dish has four small feet which raise it just above the oven shelf; this is to prevent damage to the shelf, but be guided by the manufacturer's instructions.

The browning dish can be used as a serving dish but take care not to scratch the surface. Browning dishes need not and should not be scoured, clean with a cloth and a paste made with bicarbonate of soda and water.

A browning plate is flat, surrounded by a groove. This is ideal when browning sausages or fatty foods. You can then have maximum heat while the surplus fat drains away.

Testing containers

To test if it is safe to use a certain dish in the microwave oven (excluding metal), put the dish in the microwave oven. Place a jug or glass half-filled with cold water either in or beside the dish. Microwave on HIGH for 1–2 minutes. If the dish remains cool and the water is hot, the dish is very suitable for microwaving. If the dish is slightly warm and the water is hot, the dish will also be suitable for microwaving but for shorter periods. If the dish becomes hot but the water remains cool, the dish is unsuitable for use in the microwave oven because it will absorb microwaves and could subsequently break. Dishes suitable for the microwave oven do not become hot as a result of the microwaves, but from the heat of the food being cooked in them. If cooking is for a prolonged period the dish will become very hot, so it is essential to use oven gloves to protect your hands.

Shapes of containers

A ring-shaped container will always give the best results as the microwave energy can enter from both sides as well as the top, giving more even cooking. Round containers will usually give better results than square or rectangular ones as there are no corners where over-cooking can take place. A straight-sided container is better than one with sloping sides because the depth is more even throughout. The depth of the container is equally important. Foods cooked in deep dishes cook more slowly than those in shallow dishes—choose the depth of the dish as a way of speeding up or slowing down cooking.

Microwave Cookware

Cookware	Uses	Advantages	Comments
Absorbent kitchen paper or parchment paper or freezer paper	Covering foods which splatter. Underneath foods which absorb moisture, eg thawing bread	Easily disposable.	Readily available. Wrap with shiny side toward food.
Brown paper bags	Poultry.	Holds in the heat but doesn't make food too soft; absorbs fat splashes.	
Cardboard chocolate and candy boxes	Making biscuits and cakes.	Interesting shapes often unobtainable in other materials.	Do not use if there is any metallic trimming or lettering. Line with plastic wrap.
China cups, plates and dishes	Reheating	Attractive for serving, saves washing-up.	Suitable for reheating only. Do not use metal-trimmed china.
Cling film	Covering vegetables, fish and meat dishes. Lining cake dishes.	Traps heat for faster cooking. Forms an excellent seal and is disposable. Saves washing-up.	Do not overstretch. Remove carefully to avoid steam burns. Fit loosely over the dish. Wrap double for the freezer. For prolonged cooking turn back a corner after covering.
Cooking bags	Convenience foods.	Save washing-up.	Slit on top to prevent bursting.
Corning Ware	All microwave cookery.	Interchangeable between conventional and microwave ovens, freezer and grill.	Guaranteed safe under the grill. Can be used in the freezer.
Glass ceramics	Casseroles, sauces and cakes.	Interchangeable between conventional and microwave ovens.	Avoid metal-trimmed dishes and plates.

Microwave Cookware (continued)

Cookware	Uses	Advantages	Comments
Glass jugs, heatproof	Heating liquids.		Always use a size larger than required. Do not freeze in narrow-necked jugs.
Glass, ovenproof bowls and casseroles	Bowls for sauces, custards and soups; casseroles for stews and desserts.	Easy to wash, practically unbreakable and transparent.	Avoid metal-trimmed glass. Use lids as required. Choose a larger size than you think may be needed.
Microwave browning dish or plate	Searing and sealing meat, floured fish and dry fried eggs.	Suitable for all foods where a heat-sealed surface is necessary.	Do not overheat. Use the lid when directed. Clean with bicarbonate of soda and a damp soft cloth.
Natural shells	Fish starters.	Attractive.	Suitable for short cooking only.
Ovenproof porcelain dishes	Cakes, pies and tarts.	Attractive for serving.	Cooking is sometimes slower. Avoid any metal trimming.
Paper cups	Heating drinks.	Easily disposable.	Do not use for heating oil or sugar.
Paper napkins	Heating burgers and doughnuts, warming rolls, thawing bread.	Absorb hot fat and moisture. Do not stick as much as kitchen paper.	Avoid the soft, coloured types. Do not use under dishes during prolonged cooking.
Paper plates	Reheating dry foods.	Easily disposable.	Not suitable for large quantities of food. Short-term heating only, the plates tend to lose rigidity on heating. Use double for serving.
Plastic bags, standard thickness	Brief thawing of small quantities of food from the freezer. Proving yeast doughs.	Convenient for freezer to microwave.	Remove all metal ties. Will not withstand high temperatures, so use for initial thawing only. Will not support weight of warm contents.
Plastic bags, double thickness	Freezing, thawing, and warming.		Do not use metal ties.
Plastic boxes	Initial thawing blocks of food.		Freeze with the lid on but remove lid before microwaving. Most will not withstand temperatures above 180°F (80°C) so do not freeze foods with high sugar content unless box is recommended by the manufacturer for microwave use.
Plastic cups	Heating drinks.	Disposable.	Do not boil liquid or plastic will melt.
Plastic wrap	Reheating beverages.		Avoid jugs with metal trim and those with plastic handles and handles held by metal screws.
Polyethylene bowls	Puddings, sauces and soups.	Re-usable many times. Boilable, but scar if used with hot fat or syrups.	Avoid pouring hot syrup or fat into the base. Do not use supplied lids in the microwave oven as they may be forced off by steam.
Polystyrene foam dishes	Warming food and drinks.	Disposable and easy to hold.	Will melt at high temperatures. Do not use for foods with high sugar or fat content.

Cookware	Uses	Advantages	Comments
Pottery cups, plates	Cooking and reheating		Test before using for the first time (see page 12). Avoid metal-trimmed and metallic-glazed pottery. Unglazed pottery may absorb moisture and become hot.
Pyrex (see Glass, ovenproof)			
Racks, suitable for microwave	Roasting meat and thawing where passage of air round food required.		Choose only specially made racks. Not suitable under broiler.
Roasting bags	Softening potatoes, roasting, cooking vegetables.	Hasten cooking. Aid browning.	Do not use metal ties. Remove from the oven carefully as bags are likely to burst. When liquid accumulates during cooking, place bag in a dish. Do not completely seal.
Straw baskets	Warming rolls.	Attractive for serving.	Will become brittle if heated on too many occasions or for too long.
Waxed paper	Covering foods which might pop or splutter, such as fish, chicken and baked beans.	Keeps in some of the steam while allowing the food to crisp.	Use a piece larger than the cooking dish. Secure with a toothpick to prevent the paper blowing about in the oven.
Waxed paper cartons	Reheating drinks.	Suitable for freezer to microwave.	Open carton before heating. Do not heat for too long or the carton may burst and the wax melt.
Waxed paper plates	Reheating most foods.	Do not absorb moisture.	Do not heat for long or the wax may melt.
Wine glasses	Desserts, drinks.	Attractive for serving.	Use for warming only. Delicate glasses may crack.
Wooden boards, baskets	Warming rolls.	Attractive for serving.	Wood absorbs moisture and may warp if heated for too long. No metal staples or handles in the wood.

General Look on the bottom of your everyday dishes. There will sometimes be a note that the utensil is suitable for use in the microwave oven.

You should not use plastic containers that have tightly fitting lids. Do not balance lids on the tops of containers as they will be sucked down.

Heat Controls on a Microwave Oven

There are so many different microwave ovens on the market that it would be impossible to describe the heat controls on them all. However some of the old models have only a single control which is HIGH. Others have HIGH and LOW control, the LOW one is for defrosting. Others have variable controls enabling you to move through the entire power range from HIGH, which is full power, to VERY LOW which is the equivalent of a simmer.

In this book, when food is said to be cooked on HIGH, that indicates maximum output of microwave energy and is between 600 and 700 watts. MEDIUM indicates about 60% of full power, ie 420 watts on a 700-watt oven. LOW indicates about 35% of full power. Until oven markings are standardized, you may find indicators differ from this basis.

Choosing your power setting

Most recipes can be cooked on HIGH, including vegetables, beverages, fish and bacon. Use the HIGH setting for reheating.

The MEDIUM setting can be used for all the above except when using the browning dish, which has to be on HIGH. Use the MEDIUM setting for casseroles when you have insufficient time to spare to cook on a lower setting.

Use a LOW setting for most defrosting, cooking egg and cheese mixtures, melting cheese, for casseroles using less tender meat and for softening butter.

If your oven has a WARM setting, use this for raising yeast doughs and keeping food hot. With frozen food you will have to almost double thawing times.

On some ovens the lower settings are a definite change of wattage, while on others the lower settings operate on a pulsing system so that the microwaves are on for some seconds and then switched off for a longer period of time. You can hear this on and off clicking if you listen carefully. You can make soufflés only if your oven has a LOW setting which is a continuous low wattage.

Checking your oven output

Before using any of the recipes in this book you must ascertain the output of your oven, otherwise this will affect the descriptions HIGH, MEDIUM or LOW and their timings. The output of an oven is usually about half the input. Thus if your oven is rated 1.3 kw the likely output of energy will be 600 watts. Half of the energy is used in the conversion of the electricity for microwave use.

If your oven output on HIGH is 400–450 watts you will have to allow 35% more cooking time. For ovens rated between 500 and 550 watts you need to add about 20%. These are of course only approximations. If your oven is new, look on the back or in the handbook and it will give the manufacturer's rating.

A simple, though not foolproof, test for measuring the output of your oven is as follows:

Testing your oven's output

1 Put 1 quart (1 l) water in a large ovenglass measuring jug. Record the temperature (T 1).

2 Microwave on HIGH without covering for exactly 2 minutes. Immediately record the temperature (T 2).

3 Subtract the first reading from the second reading (T 2 minus T 1) equals T 3.

4 Multiply the answer (T 3) by 19.5 for a Fahrenheit reading or 35 for a Celsius reading. Example: $T 1 = 58°F$, $T 2 = 86°F$, $T 2 - T 1 = 28$. $28 \times 19.5 = 546$. Output therefore 546 watts.

Thawing and Reheating Frozen Foods

Commercially packed foods are often frozen on styrofoam trays or in metal dishes. Remove the food from a metal dish and place in a microwave-suitable dish; remove styrofoam tray as soon as possible because it prevents the microwaves from getting through the base to thaw the meat.

Because microwaves tend to heat round the outside of the food more than in the center, you may find that the outside areas, particularly of meat, will begin to cook before the center is thawed. Overheating on the edges will be much less on the DEFROST setting.

Remember to place blocks of food in the microwave oven ice-side up; cover where possible and break up lumps as soon as they can be separated. Push still-frozen parts toward the outside of the dish, stirring as soon as it is possible. Cooked frozen food on plates can be reheated directly from the freezer. Raw foods should be thawed before cooking starts.

Reheating

Reheat most dishes, covered, on HIGH. If possible stir during cooking to distribute the heat evenly. Turn dishes which cannot be stirred and microwave for half the time on HIGH and half on LOW. Arrange the food on plates with the thick or dense parts toward the outside and the thin or more delicate parts toward the inside and try to arrange the food in an even layer.

To test whether food is sufficiently reheated, feel the bottom of the plate or dish. This should not become hot until the food is hot. Be careful when reheating sugary items such as jam-filled doughnuts because the microwaves reach the hot sugary filling first and you may burn your mouth. Take care also not to overcook food which is already well cooked, as cooking will continue during the reheating process. A little sauce added to meat will provide just that little extra moisture to prevent it from drying out.

Minestrone (page 22)

Convenience Foods

At one time or another, even the die-hard cook has to resort to using convenience foods. Take advantage of your microwave oven to speed preparation even further. Many manufacturers give microwave cooking instructions on their packages and cans. Since metal can rarely be used in the microwave oven, you must empty the food from the cans into a serving dish or plate before heating. Although foil dishes not more than $\frac{3}{4}$ inch (2 cm) deep can be used in the microwave oven, provided they are filled with food and the metal does not touch the sides of the oven, they slow down the cooking or reheating times. Cooked pies and pastries should be removed from foil dishes and reheated on a piece of parchment or freezer paper. To maintain greater crispness place this paper on a roasting rack. Use the paper and roasting rack method for thawing bread, rolls, cakes and muffins as well.

If you do not have a roasting rack elevate the bread on an upturned dish or bowl. To maintain the crispy base on a pizza brush the underneath with vegetable oil and reheat on a partly heated browning dish. Boil-in-bags must be slit and placed on a serving plate or dish before thawing and reheating.

Eggs Peperonata (page 30) in a Pyrex quiche dish from the Corningware bakeware range

Beverages

The microwave oven is faster than a kettle for boiling small quantities of water and better than a saucepan for heating milk because there is no possibility of overheated milk solids sticking to the sides of the container. If you like the feel of a saucepan you can obtain one made entirely of ovenproof glass, or a glass or pottery jug, or a cup or glass for single servings, will do. Drinks are hotter if prepared and heated in a cup, as the cup itself will heat as the liquid is warming.

Most drinks will reheat satisfactorily, although there is nothing like a fresh cup of coffee. There is no need to put both the cup and the saucer into the microwave oven but until you are able to judge exactly how long reheating or cooking will take, it is a good idea to leave both there in case it boils over. The overflow will then be contained within the saucer, making it easier to clear up.

Coffee

Coffee made with freshly ground beans can be made several hours ahead and strained into a microwave-suitable container. There are also available coffee makers specifically designed for use in the microwave oven; these usually produce filter coffee. For instant coffee, heat the water in a container or cup, then add the granules. An average cup of black coffee takes not less than 1 minute to reheat on HIGH. Two cups of black coffee take $2\frac{1}{2}$–$2\frac{3}{4}$ minutes on HIGH. Three cups (600 ml) of black coffee take $4\frac{1}{4}$–$4\frac{3}{4}$ minutes to heat on HIGH. Five cups (1.1 l) of black coffee take 7–$7\frac{1}{2}$ minutes to reheat on HIGH.

Water for tea, instant drinks or soups

1 cup ($\frac{1}{4}$ l) of cold water takes $1\frac{3}{4}$–$2\frac{1}{4}$ minutes to reach boiling point on HIGH. Two cups will take 3–$4\frac{3}{4}$ minutes; three cups (600 ml) will take 5–7 minutes; four cups ($1\frac{1}{2}$ pints) will take 8–10 minutes. Timings will vary depending on the starting temperature, the container and how many cups or mugs the larger quantities are divided between.

When drinks are only being reheated and it is not necessary to reach boiling point, less time will be required. Leave drinks to stand for a few seconds before stirring in sugar, powdered milk or coffee granules, and stir before serving.

Milk

Take care when heating milk in the microwave oven as it boils over easily. One cup will take $1\frac{3}{4}$–$2\frac{3}{4}$ minutes to reach drinking temperature on HIGH. $1\frac{1}{4}$ cups (300 ml) of milk takes $2\frac{1}{2}$–4 minutes; 3 cups (600 ml) takes 4–5 minutes. Stay near the microwave oven when heating milk and if you see it boiling up in the cup or container, quickly open the door.

Average drinking temperature is 150–160°F (65–70°C).

Defrosting frozen concentrated orange and grapefruit juice

1

Dip the unopened container into hot water to loosen the block.

2

Remove the collar and lid and tip the block of frozen concentrate into a container.

3

Microwave on HIGH for 1–$1\frac{1}{2}$ minutes, breaking the block into lumps with a plastic spatula as soon as it is possible. Stir frequently during thawing.

4

As soon as only a few lumps remain, stir well, then leave at room temperature until completely defrosted.

Supper Menu for 4 people

4 flounder fillets with Parsley Sauce (see page 92)
4 baked potatoes (see chart page 77)
4 tomatoes
2 cups (8 oz) green peas
Bread and Butter Pudding (see page 105)

40 minutes before serving
1 Make up the pudding mixture, cover and set aside.
2 Make the parsley sauce and add the parsley. Cover and set aside.
3 Prepare the potatoes. Microwave on HIGH for 12–14 minutes turning over halfway through the cooking time.
4 Meanwhile, place the fish in a shallow dish. Season; cover loosely.
5 Halve the tomatoes and arrange around the edge of a shallow dish. Season; top each with a dab of butter.
6 When the potatoes are cooked, wrap each in foil to retain its heat.
7 Cook the peas in a small bowl, adding 2 Tbsp (30 ml) salted water. Cover with plastic wrap and microwave on HIGH for 3 minutes or until cooked. Shake the bowl once during the cooking time.
8 Microwave the fish on HIGH for 3–4 minutes, turning the dish three times during cooking. Remove the cover, pour over the parsley sauce, recover and reheat on HIGH for 2 minutes until hot.
9 Drain the peas, place in the center of the dish of tomatoes. Microwave on HIGH for 3 minutes.
10 Remove the cover from the fish and the peas and tomatoes. Unwrap the potatoes and add a dab of butter or margarine. Serve hot.
11 While eating the main course, cook the pudding. Microwave on HIGH for 45 seconds, then on LOW for 12 minutes. Brown top under broiler if desired. Serve hot.

Dinner Party Menu for 4 people

Smoked Salmon, Cucumber and Shrimp Toasts (see page 41. Use half the quantity of the topping and follow the timing in the recipe)
Marinated Chicken in Teriyaki Sauce (see page 68)
10 oz (275 g) Saffron Rice (see page 87)
1 lb (450 g) sliced zucchini (see chart page 76)
green salad with French dressing
Fresh Pineapple Flambé (see page 106)
coffee
Chocolate Truffles (see page 118)

In the morning
1 Make the hollandaise sauce for the smoked salmon, cucumber and shrimp toasts. Cover with plastic wrap and leave to cool.
2 Dice the cucumber. Thaw the shrimp. Prepare the smoked salmon strips. Cover all with plastic wrap and refrigerate.
3 Cook the saffron rice by the all-in-one method (see page 87), adding a pinch of saffron. Cool and refrigerate.
4 Prepare and slice the zucchini. Place in a suitable serving dish, add 2 Tbsp (30 ml) water and a sprinkling of nutmeg. Cover with plastic wrap and refrigerate.
5 Make a French dressing, cover and set aside.
6 Prepare the salad ingredients, place in a salad bowl, cover and refrigerate.
7 Prepare the fresh pineapple slices, cover with plastic wrap and refrigerate.

2 hours before cooking
8 Prepare the marinade for the chicken in a roasting bag. Add the chicken and leave, turning the chicken occasionally.

40 minutes before serving
9 Microwave the chicken.
10 Meanwhile, finish making the topping for the smoked salmon, cucumber and shrimp toasts. Cut out 8 rounds of bread but only measuring $2\frac{1}{2}$ inches (5.5 cm). Toast, butter and complete the toppings for the toasts.
11 When the chicken is cooked, remove from the oven and leave to

stand for 10 minutes.
12 Meanwhile, microwave the zucchini on HIGH for about 8 minutes until tender. Shake the dish once or twice during the cooking time.
13 Test to see if the chicken is cooked. Slit the roasting bag down the center, remove the chicken to a warm serving dish and cover with foil. Complete the chicken sauce. Pour over the chicken and recover with foil.
14 Drain the zucchini, add a little butter if wished and cover with plastic wrap.
15 Serve the smoked salmon, cucumber and shrimp toasts, allowing 2 toasts each.
16 While eating the starter, reheat the rice, covered with plastic wrap, on HIGH for 5 minutes, stirring before serving.
17 Serve the chicken, zucchini, rice and dress the salad.
18 Cook and serve the pineapple flambé.
19 Make fresh coffee or reheat pre-prepared coffee. Serve with the truffles.

CHAPTER ONE

Stocks and Soups

All soups are tasty when freshly microwaved but are even better when they are cooked ahead, refrigerated for several hours and reheated. Add the final garnish after reheating.

Most soups can be cooked on HIGH but it is advisable to reheat on LOW those which are thickened with egg and cream. There is no need to reheat all the soup at once—a single serving reheated in a bowl will be hot in 2–3 minutes. When reheating, stir as soon as bubbles appear round the edges, then continue microwaving until they reappear and stir again. This is to avoid the possibility of your swallowing a mouthful of searing hot soup followed by a cold one.

Most soups are suitable for freezer storage, so make full use of the freezer–microwave oven combination for quick meals. Freeze in the serving quantities you are likely to need. A practical method of freezing is to pour the cold soup into a freezer bag resting upright in the bowl you will eventually use for serving. (Make sure that the bowl is freezer-proof before using this method.) Fill the bag only two-thirds full and seal it loosely at the top. Freeze until the soup is solid, then seal tightly and remove from the bowl.

To thaw, dip the bag in hot water and transfer the frozen soup to the bowl. Microwave on HIGH unless the soup has been thickened with egg, breaking up the lumps as soon as possible. If there is egg in the soup, microwave on LOW.

When there is limited freezer space it may be more practical to freeze in boxes, because they can be stacked. For thawing I usually remove the lid and up-turn the box in a bowl. Choose one that allows plenty of room for the soup to spread as it thaws. A few seconds in the microwave oven will soon loosen the block, making it easy to lift away the box. Some plastic boxes may be unsuitable for this method, particularly if the soup has a high fat content. Never try to thaw in the bag or box.

To hasten reheating, three-quarters cover the bowl with plastic wrap as soon as the frozen block of soup has separated into lumps. Thawing of soups is slow—a single serving will take at least 6 minutes to reheat on a HIGH setting. Large quantities are best thawed in a saucepan.

Stocks

It really is worth making your own stock if you enjoy wholesome soups and sauces. While bouillon cubes are very good, they do tend to add a similar flavor to every dish they are used in. Homemade stock makes use of the skins and bones that would otherwise be wasted and the only added expense is the fuel, which is considerably reduced in microwave cookery. Fish stocks are easy and trouble-free to prepare in the microwave and the fishy odor is less likely to permeate the kitchen. See Rolled Flounder Fillets in Lemon and Caper Sauce (page 37) for method.

To make stock in a microwave oven, a choice of settings is important. Not only does the MEDIUM setting prevent boiling over, but it also gives you a much better, richer stock.

Beef stock is not totally successful as it takes about 2 hours to cook in the microwave oven and even then it will not be as rich as when conventionally cooked. Considerable condensation occurs during this lengthy period and may run all over the oven shelf.

Chicken stock is much easier and is well worthwhile. Cut up the carcass and put into a 3-quart (2.8 l) ovenproof glass mixing bowl with any bones and skin. You can use the carcass and bones left over from cooked chicken, duck or turkey if you wish, or raw ones. Add a bay leaf or bouquet garni, salt and pepper and generously cover with water (as there is less evaporation when cooking by microwave you need less liquid than with the saucepan method).

Three-quarters cover the bowl with plastic wrap to hold in some of the heat and microwave on HIGH until the stock boils. If possible reduce the setting to MEDIUM for the remaining time. If your oven has no MEDIUM setting, continue cooking on HIGH. To reduce the likelihood of boiling over, make only small quantities of chicken stock on the HIGH setting. A large bowl half-filled will yield about 2½ cups (600 ml) stock and takes about 45 minutes to prepare. Strain, cool and remove the fat before using. Make larger quantities conventionally.

Packaged Soup Mixes

Reconstitute soup mixes in a large bowl according to the directions on the package but reduce the liquid by 2–3 Tbsp (30–45 ml). Three-quarters cover with plastic wrap and microwave on HIGH until boiling, stirring occasionally. $2\frac{1}{2}$ cups (600 ml) soup will take about 6 minutes, 4 cups (900 ml) 8 minutes. Stir again and cook for a further 1–2 minutes.

Clear soups with particles of vegetable or pasta should be cooked for a further 5–10 minutes on LOW.

Reheating other soups
Canned soups require reheating only. Dilute condensed soups with water as usual (not milk). Heat individual portions uncovered. Larger amounts should be reheated in a large bowl three-quarters covered with plastic wrap; stir occasionally during reheating and again just before serving and garnishing.

Reheating one individual bowl will take 2 minutes, two individual bowls 4 minutes, one large five-serving bowl 10 minutes. These times will vary according to whether the soup is clear, thick or contains vegetables or meat.

The probe temperature should be set at 160°F (70°C).

Spinach Soup

$1\frac{1}{4}$ lb (550 g) fresh spinach
3 Tbsp (40 g) butter or
   margarine
$\frac{1}{4}$ cup (40 g) all-purpose flour
$2\frac{1}{4}$ cups (450 ml) milk
$\frac{2}{3}$ cup (150 ml) chicken stock
nutmeg
salt and freshly ground pepper
1 egg yolk
3 Tbsp (45 ml) heavy cream

1

Thoroughly wash the spinach and remove the thick stems. Discard any yellow or bruised leaves.

2

Put the spinach leaves in a large roasting bag and close loosely. Stand the bag upright on the oven shelf and microwave on HIGH for 5 minutes or until the spinach is well packed down and cooked.

3

Carefully open the bag and tip the spinach and juices into a food processor or blender and blend to a smooth purée.

4

Put the butter in a 3-quart (2.8 l) ovenproof glass bowl and microwave on HIGH for 45 seconds or until melted.

5

Stir in the flour. Microwave on HIGH for 30 seconds or until the surface looks puffy.

6

Using a whisk blend in the milk. Microwave on HIGH for 2 minutes. Whisk thoroughly and continue to microwave on HIGH for 2 minutes, whisking every 30 seconds until thick.

7

Beat the spinach into the sauce and add the stock. Season with nutmeg, salt and pepper. Reheat on HIGH for 3 minutes.

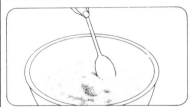

8

Stir the egg yolk into the heavy cream and add to the soup, mixing them together thoroughly.

9

Pour back into the bowl and microwave on HIGH for 30 seconds. Stir before serving.

Serves 4–6.

Tomato Soup

1 medium onion, peeled and
    quartered
3¾ cups (900 ml) tomato juice
2¼ cups (450 ml) beef stock
2 Tbsp (25 g) butter or
    margarine, softened
2 Tbsp (30 ml) all-purpose flour
1 egg yolk
2 Tbsp (30 ml) heavy cream
salt and freshly ground pepper
1 slice cooked beet, optional

1

Put the onion into a 3-quart
(2.8 l) ovenproof glass bowl. Cover
with plastic wrap, pulling back one
corner to vent, and microwave on
HIGH for 3 minutes or until the
onion is soft.

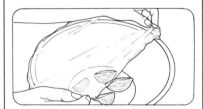

2

Stir in the tomato juice, water and
beef stock. Three-quarters cover
with plastic wrap and microwave
on HIGH for 6 minutes or until the
liquid boils round the edges. Stir
and microwave on HIGH for a
further minute.

3

While the soup is cooking blend
the butter and flour in a small bowl
until a soft paste is formed.

4

As soon as the soup is ready,
quickly add the flour paste *(beurre
manié)* in five or six pieces (it will
slither easily down the sides of the
hot mixing bowl). Carefully
remove the wrap and beat
thoroughly with a whisk. Remove
the onion. Microwave on HIGH
for 1 minute.

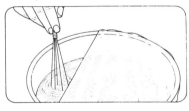

5

Blend the egg yolk and heavy
cream together and add 2–3 Tbsp
(30–45 ml) of the hot soup.

6

Return this mixture to the soup
and stir thoroughly. Season to
taste with salt and pepper and add
the beet slice.

7

Microwave on HIGH for 4 minutes
or until the soup is very hot but
not boiling. Stir occasionally
during cooking. Cover and leave
for 5 minutes; stir well before
serving.

Serves 6.

Cream of Mushroom Soup

8 oz (225 g) button mushrooms, finely chopped
$\frac{1}{4}$ onion, peeled
$2\frac{1}{2}$ cups (600 ml) hot chicken stock
$1\frac{1}{4}$ cups (300 ml) milk
3 Tbsp (40 g) butter or margarine, softened
$\frac{1}{4}$ cup (40 g) all-purpose flour
salt and freshly ground pepper
1 Tbsp (15 ml) fresh lemon juice

1

Put the mushrooms and the piece of onion in a 3-quart (2.8 l) ovenproof glass bowl, three-quarters cover with plastic wrap and microwave on HIGH for 4 minutes or until the mushrooms are soft. Stir occasionally during cooking.

2

Without removing the covering, add the stock and microwave on HIGH for 5 minutes. Cool slightly.

3

Discard the onion and purée the soup in a blender until it is smooth and creamy.

4

Pour the soup back into the bowl, add the milk and microwave on HIGH for 6 minutes or until boiling. Stir twice during cooking.

5

While the soup is reheating blend the butter with the flour to form a soft paste.

6

Add the flour and butter paste to the boiling soup in several pieces, sliding it in down the side of the hot bowl. Beat vigorously with a balloon whisk. Season to taste with salt and pepper.

7

Return the bowl of soup to the microwave oven and microwave on HIGH for 2 minutes or until the soup is bubbling. Beat again, then stir in the lemon juice

Serves 4.

Minestrone

2 small leeks, trimmed
1 carrot, peeled and cut into small dice
2 celery stalks, trimmed and finely sliced
2 Tbsp (25 g) butter or margarine
1 Tbsp (30 ml) tomato purée
pinch of garlic powder
$\frac{1}{2}$ level tsp (2.5 ml) dried basil
one $7\frac{1}{2}$-oz (213-g) can cannellini beans, drained
salt and freshly ground pepper
$\frac{1}{2}$ cup (50 g) short-cut macaroni
$\frac{1}{4}$ cup (25 g) grated Parmesan cheese

1

Cut the leeks in half lengthways, then cut each piece in half and finely slice lengthways again. Wash thoroughly in a bowl of cold water. Drain.

2

Put the prepared leeks, carrots and celery into a 3-quart (2.8 l) ovenproof glass bowl and add the butter, tomato purée, garlic powder and basil. Three-quarters cover with plastic wrap and microwave on HIGH for 15 minutes or until the carrots begin to soften. Stir two or three times during cooking.

3

Stir in $4\frac{1}{2}$ cups (1 l) boiling water, the beans and season with salt and pepper. Microwave on HIGH for 10 minutes or until the vegetables are soft, stirring once during cooking.

4

Add the macaroni. Stir thoroughly and microwave on HIGH for 5 minutes or until the pasta is tender. Stir once during cooking. Leave to stand for 5 minutes, then stir in the cheese or serve the soup offering the cheese separately.

Serves 5–6.

Note A can of kidney beans can be used instead of cannellini.

Puréed Zucchini Soup

1 lb (450 g) firm small zucchini, trimmed and finely sliced
1 large onion, peeled and very finely chopped or minced
1¼ cups (300 ml) hot chicken stock
sprig of thyme
1 tsp (5 ml) chopped chives
1 Tbsp (15 g) butter or margarine, softened
1 Tbsp (15 g) all-purpose flour
2¼ cups (450 ml) milk
salt and freshly ground pepper

1

Mix the zucchini and onion together in a 3-quart (2.8 l) ovenproof glass mixing bowl. Three-quarters cover with wrap and microwave on HIGH for 5 minutes or until the zucchini are steaming. Stir two or three times during cooking.

2

Add the hot chicken stock, sprig of thyme and chives and microwave on HIGH for 10 minutes, stirring occasionally.

3

Carefully remove the wrap, take out the thyme, then purée the mixture in a blender.

4

Pour back into the bowl, return to the microwave oven and microwave on HIGH for 2 minutes or until boiling.

5

While the purée is reheating blend the softened butter with the flour to form a soft paste. Add to the purée in small pieces allowing them to slide down the side of the hot bowl. Then beat them in thoroughly with a balloon whisk.

6

Add the milk and microwave on HIGH for 4 minutes, stirring once during cooking. Season to taste with salt and pepper. Serve hot or cold.

Serves 4.

French Onion Soup

1 lb (450 g) onions, peeled and very finely sliced
¼ cup (50 g) butter or margarine
1 level Tbsp (15 ml) all-purpose flour
3¾ cups (900 ml) beef stock
⅔ cup (150 ml) dry red wine
1 tsp (5 ml) Worcestershire sauce
salt and freshly ground pepper
4–6 slices French bread, toasted
½ cup (50 g) grated Cheddar cheese

1

Put the onions and butter in a 3-quart (2.8 l) ovenproof glass bowl and microwave on HIGH for 12 minutes. Stir occasionally during cooking.

2

Stir in the flour, then add the stock, wine and Worcestershire sauce. Three-quarters cover with wrap and microwave on HIGH for 5 minutes or until the soup begins to thicken. Stir occasionally during cooking.

3

Reduce the setting and microwave on LOW for 10 minutes.

4

Remove the bowl from the microwave oven and leave to stand. Arrange the slices of toast on a plate and sprinkle thickly with cheese. Microwave on LOW for 1½ minutes or until the cheese begins to melt.

5

Serve the soup, topping each portion with a slice of cheesy toast.

Serves 4–6.

Note The soup will be even better if stored in the refrigerator for 24 hours before reheating.

Chinese Chicken and Mushroom Soup

4 oz (125 g) cooked chicken
  breast meat, skinned
6 oz (175 g) button mushrooms
4 oz (125 g) bean sprouts,
  washed
$3\frac{3}{4}$ cups (900 ml) chicken stock
1 level tsp (5 ml) arrowroot or
  cornstarch
1 Tbsp (15 ml) dry sherry
1 tsp (5 ml) soy sauce
salt and freshly ground pepper

1

Shred the cooked chicken finely. Cut off and discard the ends of the mushroom stalks and slice the caps finely.

2

Put the chicken, sliced mushrooms and bean sprouts in a 3-quart (2.8 l) ovenproof glass bowl and stir in the stock. Three-quarters cover with wrap and microwave on HIGH for 15 minutes, stirring two or three times during cooking.

3

Blend the arrowroot, sherry and soy sauce together and mix with 2 Tbsp (30 ml) of the hot soup. Pour the mixture back into the soup and stir thoroughly. Microwave on HIGH for 5 minutes, stirring once during cooking. Season to taste with salt and pepper and stir before serving.

Serves 4

Note if desired add 1–2 Tbsp (15–30 ml) cooked rice during the last 5 minutes cooking.

Vichyssoise

1 Tbsp (15 ml) vegetable oil
1 medium onion, peeled and
  finely chopped
12 oz (350 g) potatoes, peeled
  and diced
12 oz (350 g) leeks, trimmed
  and finely shredded
$3\frac{3}{4}$ cups (750 ml) chicken stock
salt and freshly ground pepper
2 Tbsp (30 ml) sour or heavy
  cream
1 Tbsp (15 ml) chopped fresh
  parsley

1

Combine the oil and onion in a 2.8-litre (5-pint) ovenproof glass bowl and microwave on HIGH for 3 minutes or until soft. Stir once.

2

Add the potatoes and leeks to the onion. Three-quarters cover and microwave on HIGH for 5 minutes, stirring every minute

3

Add half the stock, three-quarters cover and microwave on HIGH for 4 minutes or until boiling.

4

Microwave on HIGH for a further 10 minutes or until the vegetables are soft. Cool slightly.

5

Purée in a blender, add the remaining stock and season.

6

To reheat the soup, microwave on HIGH for 3 minutes or until bubbling, stirring occasionally.

7

Just before serving stir in the soured or double cream. Garnish with chopped parsley.

Serves 6.

Golden Croûtons

2 slices white bread, crusts
  removed
butter or margarine
paprika

1

Butter the bread on both sides and cut each slice into 16 equal-sized squares.

2

Spread the croûtons out on a sheet of greaseproof paper on the oven shelf and sprinkle with paprika.

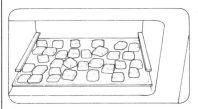

3

Microwave on HIGH for 2 minutes until the croûtons are firm but not crisp. Reposition during cooking (the croûtons will crisp during a standing time of 1–2 minutes).

4

Top each bowl of soup with 3 or 4 of the crisp, golden croûtons.

Serves 4.

Note It is essential to reposition the croûtons during cooking otherwise undisturbed pieces may overcook and burn.

CHAPTER TWO

Eggs and Cheese

Cooking eggs in the microwave oven is quick and successful and you will find it leaves you without those eggy pans to scour. Give yourself a little time to get used to the cooking methods because eggs react differently when cooked by microwave from when cooked by conventional methods.

Eggs cannot be boiled in the microwave oven because they are encased in a shell. The intense build-up of steam inside makes them burst, splattering all over the oven cavity. But you can bake eggs with the help of your microwave oven. Do not attempt to reheat a whole hard-boiled egg even without the shell as it may explode in your face as you cut into it.

When eggs are cooked by conventional methods, the whites harden before the yolks; in the microwave oven, the yolks harden before the whites. This is because microwaves are attracted to fat and the yolk has a fat content while the white does not. When the whites and yolks are beaten together, as for scrambled eggs, there is no need to take special care and they can be cooked on HIGH. Stir frequently with a fork, drawing the sides to the middle, and do not overcook. Scrambling in the microwave oven gives a greater volume than conventional scrambling because the egg does not dry in the base of the saucepan and less moisture is driven off. Scrambled eggs are ready to eat when just moist; remember they continue cooking after removal

from the oven so take care not to overcook.

A measuring cup is the easiest container to use for scrambled eggs. Microwaves cook more rapidly in a circular container and if the diameter is narrow the scrambled egg will cook with less stirring. Alternatively, an egg can be scrambled quite easily on a plate, or for a single serving I recommend a cereal or soup bowl.

When poaching, cooking without water on a plate, or in the browning dish, lightly prick the outer membrane of the yolk with a toothpick or the tip of a sharp knife and microwave on LOW. The first few times you may find that the yolk breaks and oozes through. This indicates that you have inserted the knife too deeply but you will soon master the technique.

Using the browning dish
For nice crisp-fried eggs or eggs and bacon, use the browning dish. A very lightly done egg can be cooked in the buttered browning dish simply by covering with a lid and leaving for a few moments. There will be no need to prick the yolk if cooking this way. Sometimes when eggs are poached in water or broken and cooked whole in a bed of other ingredients, such as chopped spinach, pricking is not imperative. These dishes are often cooked on MEDIUM or LOW, covered with plastic wrap or a lid.

Egg dishes such as custards, which are normally cooked in a

water bath or in a double boiler, can be cooked equally well in the microwave oven. Use a LOW setting or sit the dish in a larger dish of water and microwave on HIGH. Stir thin custard sauces frequently and reposition and turn the dishes of baked custards. Test for cooking in the usual way—a sauce should just coat the back of a spoon. To test "set" custards, insert the tip of a table knife into the custard about 1 inch (2.5 cm) from the edge. When cooked, no juices will rise to the top. The center will be soft but not runny and will cook by conduction of the heat from the outer edges during standing time.

Of course eggs are used in many other ways in cooking, such as in cakes, for binding and for coating, and no special care need be taken then. In cake making it is important to use eggs at room temperature. Do not put a whole egg (in the shell) into the microwave. If you do, it will explode. The microwave oven cannot produce a traditional dry crisp meringue but soft meringues and meringue toppings are easy to cook.

Cheese is another delicate, high protein food. It becomes stringy when overcooked, be it conventionally or by microwave, so cook egg and cheese mixtures gently and slowly using the LOW setting. Cheese can be melted on a HIGH setting if it is being used as a topping for a snack.

Scrambled Eggs

2–6 eggs
2 Tbsp (25 g) butter or
   margarine
2–5 Tbsp (30–75 ml) milk or
   milk and water
salt and freshly ground pepper
   to taste

1

Put the butter in a bowl or jug and microwave on HIGH for 45 seconds until melted. Add the milk or milk and water, salt, pepper and eggs and beat lightly together.

2

Microwave on HIGH until the egg is just set and slightly moist in the middle. Stir every 30 seconds during cooking, drawing the edges to the middle.

3

Leave to stand for 1–2 minutes before serving. Serve on hot buttered toast.

Serves 1–4.

Poached Eggs

1–4 eggs
$\frac{1}{3}$–$2\frac{1}{4}$ cups (75–450 ml) boiling
   water
$\frac{1}{4}$–1 tsp (1–5 ml) vinegar or
   lemon juice
salt

1

If cooking only 1 egg, put the boiling water, vinegar or lemon juice and a pinch of salt into a cereal bowl. If cooking more than 1 egg, put these ingredients in a 9-inch (23-cm) round shallow dish. Microwave on HIGH for 1$\frac{1}{2}$–2 minutes or until the water boils. Break each egg on to a saucer and slide it into the water.

2

Cover loosely with plastic wrap and microwave on MEDIUM for the required cooking time.

3

Leave to stand for 1 minute before uncovering (the egg will continue to cook during standing time). Remove from the water using a slotted spoon and serve on hot buttered toast.

Serves 1–4.

Although up to 4 eggs can be poached at a time in a large shallow dish, the shape of the eggs will be better if they are individually cooked in cereal bowls. The yolk and white are likely to cook at the same time if the eggs are poached on MEDIUM setting. If your oven is fitted only with a HIGH and DEFROST setting, after the water has come back to the boil, microwave a single egg on LOW and 2, 3 or 4 eggs on HIGH, reducing the cooking time by three-quarters and following with an equal rest period.

Scrambled Eggs

Eggs	Milk or mixture of milk and water	Butter or margarine	Seasoning	Cooking time
2	2 Tbsp (30 ml)		salt and freshly	1$\frac{1}{2}$–2 mins
4	4 Tbsp (60 ml)	1 Tbsp (15 g)	ground pepper	2$\frac{1}{2}$–3 mins
6	5 Tbsp (75 ml)	2 Tbsp (25 g)	to taste	3$\frac{1}{2}$–4 mins

Poached Eggs

Eggs	Boiling water	Vinegar or lemon juice	Cooking time
1	5 Tbsp (75 ml)	$\frac{1}{4}$ tsp (1.25 ml)	45 secs
2	1$\frac{1}{4}$ cups (300 ml)	$\frac{1}{2}$ tsp (2.5 ml)	1$\frac{1}{2}$ mins
3	1$\frac{1}{4}$ cups (300 ml)	$\frac{1}{2}$ tsp (2.5 ml)	2 mins
4	2$\frac{1}{4}$ cups (450 ml)	1 tsp (5 ml)	2$\frac{1}{2}$ mins

Micro-fried Egg

½ Tbsp (7 g) butter
1 egg

1

Preheat the browning dish for 3–4 minutes, slightly less than the maximum recommended by the manufacturer.

2

Add butter and, using oven gloves, tilt the browning dish so that it is evenly coated.

3

While the dish is heating, break the egg into a saucer and pierce the yolk with the tip of a sharp knife.

4

When the buttered browning dish is hot, slip the egg in as quickly as possible.

5

Cover and microwave on HIGH until the egg is nearly cooked. Leave to stand for 30 seconds before serving.
   If cooking more than 1 egg at a time, break the eggs into the corners of the dish.

For nice crisp, buttered eggs use the browning dish.

Egg and Bacon in a Browning Dish

1 egg
½ Tbsp (7 g) butter or margarine
2 strips bacon

1

Preheat the browning dish to the maximum recommended by the manufacturer. While the browning dish is heating, break the egg into a saucer and prick through the outer membrane of the yolk with the tip of a sharp knife. Snip the bacon fat at intervals.

2

When the browning dish is ready add the butter and quickly put in the bacon strips, arranging them around the edge of the dish. Microwave on HIGH for 30 seconds, then turn bacon over.

3

Slide the egg into the center of the dish, then cover with the lid and microwave on HIGH for 30 seconds or until the egg is nearly cooked. Leave to stand, covered, for 1 minute before serving.

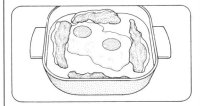

Serves 1.

Note For 2 eggs and 4 strips of bacon, increase the cooking time to 45 seconds in steps 3 and 4.

Egg and Bacon in an Ordinary Dish

2 strips bacon
1 egg

1

Snip the bacon fat at intervals so that it will lie flat on the dish. Arrange the bacon strips on either side of a shallow dish and cover with paper towels. Microwave on HIGH for 1½ minutes or until the bacon is almost cooked.

2

Break the egg into a saucer and pierce through the outer membrane of the yolk with the tip of a sharp knife.

3

Slide the egg between the bacon strips, cover with plastic wrap and microwave on HIGH for 45 seconds or until the egg is nearly cooked.

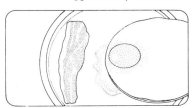

4

Leave to stand for 1–2 minutes before removing the wrap.

Serves 1.

Note It is better to cook the egg and bacon in a dish rather than a plate so that the plastic wrap is not in direct contact with the egg yolk.

Baked Eggs with Frankfurters and Mushrooms

$\frac{1}{2}$ **Tbsp (7 g) butter or**
margarine
3 regular frankfurters, cut into
$\frac{1}{2}$**-inch (1-cm) slices**
$\frac{1}{3}$ **cup (75 g) button**
mushrooms, roughly
chopped
salt and freshly ground pepper
4 eggs
$\frac{2}{3}$ **cup (150 ml) heavy cream**

1

Put the butter in a 9-inch (23-cm) round shallow dish and microwave on HIGH for 45 seconds or until melted.

2

Add the frankfurters and mushrooms and microwave on HIGH for 4 minutes or until the mushrooms are soft. Stir two or three times during cooking. Drain. Season with pepper and add salt sparingly.

3

Leaving a border of frankfurter mushroom mixture, make four wells in the mixture and break an egg into each.

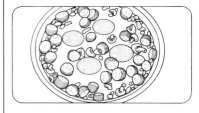

4

Pour the cream evenly over the mixture, being sure to coat the eggs completely. Reduce the setting, cover and microwave on LOW for 7 minutes or until the egg whites are on the point of setting. Give the dish a quarter-turn three times during cooking.

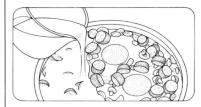

5

Leave to stand for 5 minutes before uncovering to enable the eggs to finish cooking.

Serves 4.

Note For variation, substitute any variety of salami or chopped ham.

Welsh Rarebit

2 Tbsp (30 ml) milk
1 egg yolk
$\frac{1}{4}$ **level tsp (1.25 ml) dry mustard**
pinch of pepper
4 oz (125 g) Cheddar cheese,
grated
2 slices bread
butter

1

In a medium bowl blend the milk and egg yolk together. Then add the mustard and pepper and mix thoroughly.

2

Gently stir in the grated cheese and microwave on LOW for 1$\frac{1}{2}$ minutes or until the cheese is partially melted. Stir twice during cooking (under rather than over-cook or the cheese will become stringy).

3

Toast and lightly butter the bread and leave the grill switched on.

4

Pile half the cheese mixture on to each slice of toast and quickly brown under the grill.

Serves 2.

Note Double the mixture for 4 servings, microwaving on LOW for about 3 minutes. If you prefer not to brown the cheese, top the Welsh rarebit with sliced tomatoes, mushrooms, strips of ham or chopped corned beef. To cook sliced tomatoes and mushrooms, see pages 76 to 77.

Spanish Omelette

1 Tbsp (15 g) butter or
  margarine
½ small green pepper, seeded
  and thinly sliced
½ small red pepper, seeded and
  thinly sliced
1 small onion, peeled and
  chopped
1 small potato, cooked and
  diced
3 eggs
2 Tbsp (30 ml) milk or water
salt and freshly ground pepper

1

Put the butter in a 9-inch (23-cm) shallow pie dish and microwave on HIGH for 45 seconds until melted.

2

Add the green and red peppers and onion, cover with plastic wrap and microwave on HIGH for 3 minutes until soft.

3

Add the diced, cooked potato to the vegetables in the pie dish and stir to mix.

4

Beat the eggs, milk or water and seasoning together and pour into the dish. Cover loosely with wrap and microwave on LOW for a further 3 minutes, until the omelette is set.

5

Carefully remove the plastic wrap and brown quickly under a hot grill.

Serves 2.

Note You can vary the filling by, instead of potato in step 2, adding grated cheese, cooked mushroom slices, chopped ham, cooked chopped bacon or tuna fish.

Puffy Omelette

1 Tbsp (15 g) butter or
  margarine
3 eggs, separated
3 Tbsp (45 ml) milk
¼ level tsp (1.25 ml) salt
¼ level tsp (1.25 ml) white
  pepper

1

Put the butter in a 9-inch (23-cm) round dish and microwave on HIGH for 45 seconds or until melted. Tilt the dish so that the surface is completely covered with butter.

2

In a large bowl lightly beat the egg yolks, milk, salt and pepper together. Using clean beaters and a grease-free bowl, whisk the egg whites until stiff.

3

Stir 1 Tbsp (15 ml) of the egg whites into the milk mixture, then fold in the remainder (do not over-mix). Pour into the buttered dish and microwave on LOW for 5 minutes or until the foam is only just set. Quickly and without causing a draught, open the oven door and give the dish a quarter-turn three times during cooking.

4

While the omelette is cooking, light the grill and heat to maximum. After the omelette is cooked leave to stand for a minute, then slide on to a flameproof plate, folding over at the same time. Brown under the grill.

Serves 2.

Eggs Peperonata

1 Tbsp (15 ml) vegetable oil
2 large onions, peeled and
  finely chopped
1 level tsp (5 ml) all-purpose
  flour
1 lb (450 g) tomatoes, peeled
  and sliced
1 red pepper, seeded and thinly
  sliced into rings
1 green pepper, seeded and
  thinly sliced into rings
salt and freshly ground pepper
4 eggs

1

Combine the oil and onion in a
10-inch (25-cm) round shallow dish
and microwave on HIGH for 3
minutes or until the onion is soft.
Stir occasionally during cooking.

2

Stir in the flour, then add the
tomatoes and peppers and season
with salt and pepper.

3

Three-quarters cover with plastic
wrap and microwave on HIGH for
7 minutes or until the peppers are
soft. Stir gently occasionally during
cooking.

4

Make four wells in the vegetable
mixture and arrange a slice of red
or green pepper in each. Break an
egg into each well.

5

Completely cover with plastic
wrap and microwave on LOW for
7 minutes or until the egg white is
on the point of setting. Give the
dish a quarter-turn three times
during cooking. Leave to stand for
5 minutes before removing the
cover. Serve a portion of
peperonata with each egg.

Serves 4

Crispy Hot Cheese Sandwich

4 slices bread
2 slices processed cheese
butter or margarine

1

Preheat the browning dish to
maximum according to the
manufacturer's instructions.

2

Meanwhile sandwich the bread
with the cheese, then spread the
butter on the outside of the
sandwiches.

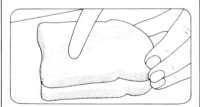

3

Immediately the browning dish is
ready, put in the sandwiches,
pressing down with a fish slice.
Leave for 15 seconds then turn
over and microwave on HIGH for
10 seconds or until cheese has
melted. Do not cover during
cooking. Serve immediately.

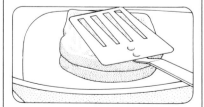

Serves 2.

Note One sandwich can be
cooked in the same way.

Ham and Cheese Snack

2 slices Gruyère cheese
4 slices ham
½ egg, beaten
2 Holland rusks, finely crushed

1

Sandwich the cheese between two
slices of ham, then dip in the
beaten egg and coat with the
crumbs.

2

Put on small individual plates,
cover with waxed paper and
microwave each on HIGH for 1
minute or until the cheese is
melted.

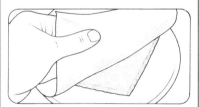

Serves 2.

Note For a really convenient
snack use square slices of ham
which are available in vacuum
packs.

CHAPTER THREE

Fish and Shellfish

Fish fillets, steaks and whole fish can all be cooked by microwave and served simply or dressed up with sauces. Use the microwave oven for all methods of fish cookery except frying. Deep frying in the microwave oven is extremely dangerous and shallow frying is not possible, but you can simulate frying by coating fish in egg and crumbs and microwaving in 1 Tbsp (15 ml) oil.

Fish tastes excellent when cooked by microwave because it retains its natural juices. It cooks fast and reheats well and so is a good stand-by for latecomers or when you want to prepare a dinner party starter which can be done in advance. But be sure not to overcook fish in the microwave oven, as cooking continues during a brief standing time.

Cooking whole fish

To cook whole fish, first slash the skin in several places to prevent it bursting. Place in a dish in a single layer, overlapping the thinner parts and arranging them toward the center. Insert small pieces of plastic wrap between overlapping parts to keep them separate. When cooking more than two fish, use a square or oblong dish and move the outside fish to the middle halfway through cooking. Large fish should also be turned over once during cooking. Cover the heads and tails with small pieces of smooth foil as soon as they are cooked. As a general guide allow about 4 minutes per 1 lb (450 g).

Whole fish which are too big to fit into the oven straight can be curved into a round dish or cooked directly on a turntable. Loosely join the head and tail with string. Remember you cannot straighten the fish once it is cooked.

Steaks and pieces

To cook steaks or large pieces of fish, arrange them in a single layer of even thickness. Arrange any thin parts toward the center and overlapping. Keep overlapping parts separated with small pieces of plastic wrap. Cover steaks during cooking because the parts near the bone cook quickly and splatter.

Fillets can be cooked flat or they can be rolled, which enables you to cook more pieces at once. Fillets and small pieces of fish should be repositioned or gently stirred during cooking.

Shellfish

Shellfish can also be cooked by microwave but timing is important as overcooking causes them to toughen. Test frequently to see whether they are done. If cooking lobster, kill it first; death may not be immediate in the microwave oven, as it is not possible to get a large enough container of boiling water inside.

Thawing fish and shellfish

Frozen fish and shellfish should be thawed before cooking by microwave. Remove the fish from the wrapper and put in a dish or on a plate. Microwave on LOW, turning and repositioning the fish frequently. Fillets should be separated as soon as the top one softens. While waiting for the center parts to thaw, the edges may start to cook; so as soon as the edges are pliable, finish thawing in cold water.

It is easy to see when fillets or steaks are thawed because the glassy appearance disappears, but it is more difficult to judge whole fish, since you cannot see into the center. Pierce with a skewer in the thickest part and if there is resistance allow more time.

Small pieces, such as shelled scallops, should be arranged in a circle and covered with paper towels. Remove any that are nearly thawed to avoid accidental cooking. Complete thawing in cold water.

Boil-in-the-bag fish

Boil-in-the-bag fish should have the bag pierced before cooking.

Breaded fish fillets

Although it isn't possible to fry in the microwave oven, fish coated in golden crumbs will be very appetizing indeed.

Accompanying sauces

Fresh fish to so tasty when cooked simply that a sauce may seem unnecessary. Garnish plain fish with chopped fresh parsley, chives, lemon wedges, watercress sprigs, browned breadcrumbs or a savory butter.

Baked Fish

1 whole fish, up to 2 lb (900 g)
  in weight, cleaned
salt and freshly ground pepper
butter, softened

1

Slash the skin 3 times on each side
to allow for even cooking. Rub salt
and pepper into the skin. Spread
both sides with butter, about
1 oz (25 g) to a 1-lb (450-g) fish.

2

Place in a shallow dish in which the
fish just fits. Cover with plastic
wrap and microwave on HIGH for
3 minutes per 1 lb (450 g) or until
the fish is tender.

3

After 3 minutes, turn the fish over
and reposition it, if possible. Cover
the head and tail with smooth
pieces of foil to prevent them from
becoming dry and brittle. Be
careful to place the foil so that it
will stay within the perimeter of
the dish. To test, insert a fork into
the thickest part of the fish. If it
does not flake easily allow a little
longer cooking time. Garnish and
serve.

Serves 1–2.

Note This recipe is suitable for
sea trout, whiting, mackerel,
mullet, trout, carp, cod or
haddock. It is not suitable for
flounder and lemon sole.

Baked Whole Flat Fish

1 large flounder or lemon sole
  weighing 14 oz (400 g) after
  cleaning
softened butter or soft
  margarine
salt and freshly ground pepper

1

Slash the skin 3 times on each side
to allow even cooking. Butter the
dark skin of the fish and place this
side down in a shallow dish in
which the fish just fits.

2

Season the fish with salt and
pepper and butter liberally over
the white skin.

3

Without covering, microwave on
HIGH for 2 minutes or until the
tail end is cooked. Give the dish a
half-turn.

4

Cover the cooked end of the tail
with a small piece of foil and
microwave on HIGH for 1 minute
or until the wide end is cooked.
To test, insert the tip of a sharp
knife into one of the slits in the
skin and through to the underside
of the dish. The flesh should be
white. Garnish and serve.

Serves 1.

Note The flounder is left
uncovered because the skin, which
may be tough to eat, protects the
delicate flesh, keeping it moist and
flavorsome. Remove the skin
before serving if you wish.

Baking Two Large Fish

2 whole fish, up to 2 lb (900 g)
  in weight, cleaned

1

Prepare the fish as in step 1 of
Baked Fish (left). Arrange each fish
in 2 identical shallow oblong
dishes. Cover with plastic wrap.
Place the dishes one on top of the
other at right angles. Microwave
on HIGH for 1 minute.

2

Reverse the dishes top to bottom,
giving each a quarter-turn. Cover
the tail ends, if cooked, with
smooth pieces of foil. Continue to
cook, reversing the dishes every 2
minutes for a further 7 minutes or
until both fish are cooked.
Calculate the cooking time at
about 4 minutes to 1 lb (450 g) total
fish weight.

Baking four fish
Three-quarters cook the first pair
and set them aside while
completely cooking the second
pair. Remove the dishes from the
oven and complete the cooking of
the first pair. Garnish and serve.

**Kipper Pâté (page 36) and
Smoked Salmon, Cucumber
and Prawn Toasts (page 41)**

Baked White Fish Steaks or Fillets

steaks or fillets of cod,
    haddock, flounder, sole,
    whiting, hake, carp or tilefish
salt and white pepper
butter or margarine (optional)
lemon juice (optional)

1

Season the fish to taste with salt and white pepper, butter if desired and sprinkle with lemon juice if liked.

2

Arrange in a single layer in a shallow dish. Place the thicker parts of fillets toward the outside, overlapping the thin ends and separating them with plastic wrap or non-stick paper.

3

Cover the dish loosely with plastic wrap or waxed paper and microwave on HIGH for 4 minutes per 1 lb (450 g).

4

Turn steaks over and reposition three times during cooking. For fillets, give the dish a quarter-turn three times during cooking.

Fresh Salmon with Sauce Maltaise (page 38) in a Corningware French white dish

Baked Smoked Haddock, Cod or Kippers

smoked haddock (on the bone
    or filleted), or smoked cod
    or kippers, or smoked
    whitefish or chubb

1

Wash the fish and place skin side down in a shallow dish. Cover loosely with plastic wrap.

2

Microwave on HIGH for 4 minutes per 1 lb (450 g), giving the dish a quarter-turn three times during cooking.

3

Test the fish and if it does not flake easily, allow a little longer cooking time. Leave to stand for 5 minutes before uncovering.

Note Kipper fillets may be cooked in two layers separated with plastic wrap in the same dish, and repositioned during cooking.

Baked Smoked Mackerel, Trout or Eel

whole or filleted smoked
    mackerel, trout or eel
lemon juice (optional)
softened butter or soft
    margarine

1

Put the fish into a shallow dish that just fits them. Overlap the tails or thinner parts, separating them with plastic wrap, to make an even layer of fish.

2

Sprinkle with lemon juice if liked and spread with softened butter allowing about 1 Tbsp (15 g) to 1 lb (450 g) fish.

3

Cover loosely with plastic wrap and microwave on HIGH for 2 minutes or until hot. Serve the fish with the juices from the dish poured over.

Note If you prefer smoked fish to taste less salty, place a few tablespoons of water in the dish before starting to cook. These are ready to eat cold and simply need re-heating.

Browned Baked Fish

whole fish, up to 8 oz (225 g) weight, such as trout, mackerel, herring or snapper
butter or margarine
salt and freshly ground pepper

1

For one 8-oz (225-g) fish, preheat a small browning dish according to the manufacturer's instructions, adding about 1 Tbsp (15 g) butter for the last 30 seconds.

2

Meanwhile cut the skin 3 times on each side of the fish. Rub with salt and pepper.

3

Without removing the dish from the oven, turn the fish quickly in the brown, sizzling butter. Microwave, uncovered, on HIGH for 2 minutes.

4

Turn the fish over carefully and reposition. Microwave on HIGH for 1 minute or until cooked. For 2 fish allow 4–5 minutes cooking, turning once. For 4 fish allow 7–8 minutes cooking; turn and reposition after 3 minutes.

Browned Fish Steaks or Fillets

fillets of fish, up to 8 oz (225 g) weight, such as cod, haddock, whiting, tilefish, red snapper or salmon, washed and patted dry
butter or margarine
seasoned flour for coating

1

Preheat a browning dish according to the manufacturer's instructions adding about 1 Tbsp (15 g) butter for the last 30 seconds. Meanwhile, lightly coat the fillets in seasoned flour.

2

Turn the fish quickly in the brown sizzling butter, then, with the skin, sides uppermost if appropriate, microwave, uncovered, on HIGH, cooking thin fillets for 1 minute, steaks for 2 minutes.

3

Turn the fish over carefully and reposition. Microwave on HIGH for 2 minutes or until tender.

Poached Whole Fish

1–2 lb (450–900 g) fish
1–2 stalks celery, washed and sliced
1 small onion, peeled and sliced
1 carrot, peeled and sliced
1 large tomato, peeled and seeded (optional)
chopped fresh herbs, such as parsley, chervil, dill
salt and freshly ground pepper
2 Tbsp (30 ml) fresh lemon or lime juice, or flavored vinegar
4 Tbsp (60 ml) water or wine

1

Wash the fish and dry on paper towels. Put the prepared vegetables and herbs into a dish that the fish will just fit. Season the fish and place on top of the vegetables.

2

Add the lemon or lime juice or flavored vinegar and water or wine. Cover loosely with plastic wrap and microwave on HIGH for 5–7 minutes or until tender, turning the fish after 3 minutes cooking. Leave covered to stand for 3 minutes before serving.

3

The vegetables can be served with the fish or puréed in a blender and reheated with a pat of butter to serve as a sauce.

Note *For mild fish steaks and fillets*, add milk or water and a little butter to the liquid. When strained from the fish after cooking, the liquid can be used in making a sauce.
   Suitable for whole fish up to 2 lb (900 g) weight after cleaning. Choose fish such as trout, mackerel, whiting, snapper, mullet, halibut, haddock, bass, herring, carp, or turbot. The method is also suitable for steaks and fillets such as cod, haddock, hake, carp, salmon, flounder and sole.

Crispy Crumbed Fillets

1 lb (450 g) fish fillets, such as cod, haddock, whiting, perch
1 Tbsp (15 ml) vegetable oil
2 Tbsp (25 g) butter or margarine
salt and freshly ground pepper
1 egg, beaten
breadcrumbs

1

Cut the fish into portions that will fit easily into the dish allowing room for quick turning over.

2

Sprinkle the fillets with salt and pepper, dip in beaten egg and breadcrumbs and pat with a knife to press the crumbs well into the surface.

3

Preheat the browning dish to maximum according to the manufacturer's instructions, adding the oil and butter during the last 30 seconds.

4

As soon as the dish is hot, use oven mitts to tilt the dish so that the surface is evenly coated with fat.

5

Quickly put the fish into the prepared browning dish, placing the best-looking side downward. Microwave on HIGH for 2 minutes, then turn the fish over, giving the dish a half-turn at the same time. Cook for a further 2 minutes or until the fish is cooked. Drain.

Micro-fried Fish

1 Tbsp (15 ml) vegetable oil
1 lb (450 g) flaked fish fillets

1

Put 1 Tbsp (15 ml) vegetable oil in a large shallow dish and microwave on HIGH for 1 minute.

2

Add the prepared fillets, remembering that the side that is placed underneath will be the one that shows when the fish is served up and will be the better side. Microwave on HIGH allowing about 4 minutes per 1 lb (450 g).

3

Turn the fish over and give the dish a half-turn once during cooking.

Note The coating on flaked fish cooked in an ordinary dish will be acceptable but not crisp.

Fish Sticks

1 Tbsp (15 ml) vegetable oil
frozen fish sticks

1

Preheat a browning dish to maximum according to the manufacturer's instructions, adding the oil during the last 20 seconds.

2

Using oven mitts, quickly tilt the dish to completely coat the surface with the oil and put in the fish sticks. Microwave on HIGH for 20 seconds per fish stick, then flip the fish sticks over, repositioning them in the dish, and microwave on HIGH for a further 10–15 seconds (the length of time depends on the starting temperature of the fish).

3

Leave to stand for 2–3 minutes before serving.

Note Starting temperatures of frozen fish vary, so watch the cooking carefully. Undercooking can be remedied—overcooking cannot! Fish sticks can be cooked from frozen in the microwave oven on a well-greased ordinary plate—but they will not be crisp. Ten fish sticks will take about 3 minutes on HIGH, 4 fish sticks take about 2 minutes. A better result is obtained using the browning dish.

Mackerel or Bluefish à l'Orange

2 Tbsp (25 g) butter
1 medium orange, peeled,
   segmented and chopped
2 sprigs of mint
two 6-oz (175-g) mackerel or
   bluefish, cleaned
salt and freshly ground pepper

1

Put the butter in a shallow dish which will just take the fish arranged in a single layer and microwave on HIGH for 1 minute or until melted.

2

Stir in the chopped orange and the mint. Cover with waxed paper and microwave on HIGH for 2 minutes, stirring after 1 minute.

3

Slash the skin of the mackerel or bluefish in two or three places and season with salt and pepper.

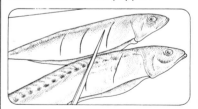

4

Place in the dish side by side, cover with waxed paper and microwave on HIGH for 2 minutes.

5

Turn the fish over, re-cover and microwave on HIGH for 2 minutes or until the fish is cooked.

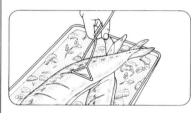

6

To serve, remove the sprigs of mint and spoon the orange over the fish.

Serves 2.

Note Trout are also very good cooked this way.
   To cook 4 fish, double the quantities, allowing half to three-quarters as much time again at each stage of cooking. When turning them over, reposition so that the outside fish are placed in the middle.

Kipper or Smoked Whitefish Pâté

1 lb (450 g) kipper or whitefish
   fillets
½ cup (125 g) unsalted butter at
   room temperature
2 Tbsp (30 ml) lemon juice
1 level tsp (5 ml) paprika
2 Tbsp (30 ml) heavy cream
freshly ground black pepper
black olives and lemon slices,
   to garnish

1

Arrange the fish fillets in a shallow dish (this can be done in a double layer provided they are separated by a sheet of plastic wrap), or cut up the fillets to fit the dish.

2

Cover the dish and microwave on HIGH for 3–4 minutes or until the fish is cooked. Give the dish a half-turn halfway through cooking. Remove the skin and any bones from the fish.

3

Cut the butter into four pieces, and purée with the fish, the lemon juice and paprika in a blender or food processor. Then quickly blend in the heavy cream and pepper to taste.

4

Spoon the mixture into individual or one large serving dish and decorate with black olives and lemon slices. Chill.

5

Remove from the refrigerator about 30 minutes before serving. Serve with thin slices of freshly toasted brown bread.

Serves 6–8.

Note This fish pâté freezes well without the garnish.

Smoked Fish à la Crème

1½ lb (750 g) smoked haddock or
  shad fillet
2 Tbsp (25 g) butter or
  margarine, softened
2 Tbsp (15 g) all-purpose flour
1¼ cups (300 ml) milk
½ cup (125 ml) heavy cream
1 Tbsp (15 ml) chopped fresh
  parsley, or 1 level tsp (5 ml)
  dried parsley
2 hard-boiled eggs, chopped
freshly ground pepper
salt (optional)

1

Cut up the fish fillet if necessary and put in a dish in which it just fits. Cover loosely with plastic wrap and microwave on HIGH for 6 minutes or until cooked. Give the dish a quarter-turn during cooking.

2

While the fish is cooking, blend the butter and flour together in a small bowl to form a soft paste.

3

Remove the fish from the dish. Flake the flesh and discard all skin and bones.

4

Stir the milk and cream into the juices left in the dish and microwave on HIGH for 4 minutes or until boiling, stirring twice during cooking.

5

Gradually add the liquid to the flour and butter paste, beating thoroughly, then stir in the parsley. Microwave on HIGH for 1 minute or until the sauce thickens and just boils. Stir twice during cooking.

6

Stir the flaked fish and the hard-boiled eggs into the sauce and microwave on LOW for 4 minutes or until reheated. Stir occasionally during cooking.

7

Season with pepper, adding salt only if necessary. Serve with vegetables of your choice.

Serves 4.

Note If you are cooking whole smoked haddock, remember that a 1½ lb (750 g) fish will yield only about 1 lb (450 g) edible flesh. Always reheat fish in sauce dishes on a LOW setting.

Soused Herrings

4 herrings, filleted
salt and freshly ground pepper
⅔ cup (150 ml) wine vinegar
6 peppercorns
2 bay leaves
1 onion, peeled and very thinly
  sliced

1

Put the fillets flat and skin side down on a board. Sprinkle the flesh side with salt and pepper.

2

Roll up the fish starting from the head end and secure with wooden toothpicks. Arrange in a single layer in a shallow square or round dish.

3

Combine the vinegar, ⅔ cup (150 ml) water, the peppercorns, bay leaves and onion rings in a bowl and microwave on HIGH for 2 minutes or until the mixture boils.

4

Pour over the herrings, cover and microwave on HIGH for 5 minutes or until the fish is cooked. Give the dish a half-turn halfway through cooking.

5

Turn the fish over carefully in the liquid, cover and leave to cool before refrigerating.

Serves 4.

Note You can also use this recipe for small mackerel. Larger fillets can be cut in two lengthways and rolled up in the same way. They can be kept in the refrigerator for up to 4 days.

Rolled Flounder Fillets in Lemon and Caper Sauce

2 lb (900 g) flounder fillets, with skin
salt and freshly ground pepper
2 Tbsp (25 g) butter or margarine
2 level Tbsp (30 ml) all-purpose flour
1 Tbsp (15 ml) lemon juice
1 Tbsp (15 ml) capers
2 egg yolks
chopped fresh parsley and lemon wedges to garnish

1

To make a quick fish stock: skin the flounder and put them in a medium bowl. Just cover with water and microwave on HIGH until the mixture boils. Stir, reduce the setting and microwave on LOW for 5 minutes. Strain.

2

Cut the fillets of flounder in half lengthways and season lightly with salt and pepper. Roll up head to tail and arrange in a shallow dish. Cover and microwave on HIGH for 4 minutes, then reposition the fish and microwave on HIGH for 2 minutes or until the fish is just cooked. Spoon the juices from the flounders into a measuring cup. Set the fish aside, covered, while making the sauce.

3

Make the juices up to 1 cup (225 ml) with the prepared fish stock. Put the butter in a large cup or bowl and microwave on HIGH for 45 seconds or until melted. Stir in the flour, then add the fish juices and stock.

4

Add the lemon juice and capers and season to taste with salt and pepper. Microwave on HIGH for 1 minute, then stir and continue microwaving until the mixture boils and thickens slightly.

5

Beat the egg yolks with 1 Tbsp (15 ml) cold water and stir into the sauce. Reduce the setting and microwave on LOW for 2 minutes, or until the sauce thickens. Stir once during cooking.

6

Pour the sauce over the fish and without covering microwave on HIGH for 1 minute or until reheated. Serve hot, garnished with chopped fresh parsley and lemon wedges.

Serves 4–5.

Note For stronger flavored fish stocks, add bones, heads if they are small, herbs, small pieces of onion, celery, carrot, and some salt and pepper. The bones and skin from 2 lb (900 g) fish, well covered with cold water, will take about 5 minutes on HIGH to reach boiling point. Reduce the setting to LOW for the remainder of cooking time. The bowl should not be more than one-third full and should be left uncovered.

Fresh Salmon with Sauce Maltaise

four 4–6 oz (125–175 g) slices fresh salmon
salt and freshly ground pepper
3 Tbsp (40 g) butter, softened

For the sauce maltaise
1 small orange
½ cup (125 g) unsalted butter
4 Tbsp (60 ml) heavy cream
3 egg yolks
¼ level tsp (1.25 ml) salt
¼ level tsp (1.25 ml) white pepper

1

Season the salmon with salt and pepper and spread on both sides with butter.

2

Arrange in a single layer in a narrow dish, the ends tucked inward toward the center.

3

Cover with waxed paper (salmon tends to pop during cooking) and microwave on LOW for 8–12 minutes or until the fish is just cooked. Turn the fish over and give the dish a half-turn, halfway through cooking.

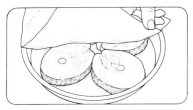

4

Cover the dish tightly and leave to stand while preparing the sauce.

Aromatic Poached Halibut Steaks

For the court bouillon
1 cup (240 ml) dry white wine
1 medium carrot, peeled and
    finely chopped
1 celery stalk, scraped and
    finely chopped
1 medium onion, peeled and
    finely chopped
2 bay leaves

6 crushed peppercorns
4 sprigs parsley
1 level tsp (5 ml) salt
grated rind of 1 lemon
1 tsp (5 ml) lemon juice

four to six 1-inch (2-cm)-thick
    halibut steaks, about 2 lb
    (900 g), cut from the tail end
    of the fish

5

To prepare the sauce, cut 1 slice from the orange and reserve for garnishing. Finely grate the rind from the orange and squeeze out the juice. Put the butter in a medium bowl and microwave on HIGH for 1 minute or until melted.

6

Add the orange rind and juice and the remaining ingredients and whisk until smooth.

7

Microwave on HIGH for 1 minute, beating briskly with a balloon whisk every 15 seconds. Continue to cook on LOW for 2–3 minutes or until the sauce thickens, whisking frequently.

8

Pour a little sauce over the top of each slice. Then garnish with the orange slice.

Note Remember to beat the sauce frequently and vigorously to ensure emulsification and prevent curdling. Do not attempt to make a smaller quantity of sauce as the timing, which is critical, will be too short to control. The sauce may be frozen and thawed gently in the microwave oven, beating frequently. The consistency of the sauce depends upon the size of the orange used.

1

Put all the court bouillon ingredients with 2 cups (425 ml) water into a large deep casserole. Cover with the lid and microwave on HIGH for 8 minutes or until the liquid is boiling.

2

Uncover and gently lower in the fish steaks. Replace the lid and microwave on HIGH for 3 minutes or until the liquid starts to bubble.

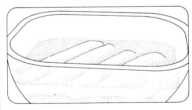

3

Continue microwaving on HIGH for 1–2 minutes or until the liquid bubbles again. Give the dish a half-turn halfway through cooking. Microwave on HIGH for a further 1 minute or until the flesh can easily be separated from the bone and is opaque in the center.

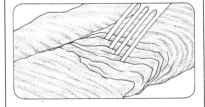

4

Replace the lid after testing and leave to stand for 5 minutes. Remove the fish carefully with a slotted spoon. Serve hot with melted butter.

5

The fish is equally delicious cold and, if serving this way, it should be left in the liquid until it is completely cold, then well drained and served with mayonnaise.

Serves 4–6.

Note This recipe is equally good when cooking expensive cuts such as salmon or cheaper cuts such as cod or haddock steaks. It improves the flavor of frozen fish steaks too; these should be thawed and drained before adding to the bouillon.

Fish Balls in Cucumber Sauce

1 lb (450 g) white fish fillet, minced
2 medium onions, peeled and grated or finely chopped
1 small carrot, peeled and grated
$\frac{1}{2}$ cup (50 g) fresh white breadcrumbs
$\frac{1}{2}$–1 level tsp (2.5–5 ml) salt
$\frac{1}{4}$ level tsp (1.25 ml) white pepper
1 egg, beaten

For the sauce
1 small cucumber, topped, tailed, but not peeled, then puréed in a blender or finely chopped
about 1 cup (225 ml) fish or chicken stock
$\frac{1}{4}$ cup (50 g) butter or margarine
1 small garlic clove, peeled and crushed
$\frac{1}{4}$ cup (50 g) all-purpose flour
1 level tsp (1.25 ml) ground bay leaf
2 Tbsp (30 ml) heavy cream
salt and freshly ground pepper

1

To make the fish balls, combine the minced fish, onions, carrot, breadcrumbs, salt and pepper and bind with the beaten egg.

2

Divide the fish mixture into 16 pieces and form into balls, using wet cold hands.

3

Arrange the fish balls in a large shallow dish. Cover and microwave on HIGH for 6 minutes, repositioning and turning the balls over once halfway through cooking.

4

To make the sauce, measure the cucumber purée and make up to 2$\frac{1}{2}$ cups (600 ml) with stock.

5

Put the butter in a medium bowl, add the garlic and microwave on HIGH for 45 seconds or until the butter is melted. Add the flour, ground bay leaf and the cucumber liquid.

6

Microwave on HIGH for 3 minutes or until the sauce thickens, whisking twice during cooking. Stir in the cream and season to taste with the salt and pepper.

7

Pour over the fish and without covering, microwave on LOW for 8 minutes or until reheated. Give the dish a half-turn halfway through cooking.

Serves 6–8.

Note If wished, the fish balls can be prepared in advance. Arrange in the dish, cover and refrigerate. Bring back to room temperature before cooking.

Lobster Thermidor

3 Tbsp (40 g) butter
1 small onion, peeled and finely chopped
2 small or 1 large lobster, cooked, or 12 oz (350 g) cooked lobster meat
3 Tbsp (45 ml) dry white wine
1 level tsp (5 ml) Dijon-style mustard
1$\frac{1}{4}$ cups (300 ml) Béchamel Sauce, coating consistency (page 93)
6 level Tbsp (90 ml) grated Gruyère cheese
2 level Tbsp (30 ml) grated Parmesan cheese
1 egg yolk

1

Put the butter and onion in a large shallow dish and microwave on HIGH for 2 minutes until the onion is softened.

2

Stir in the lobster meat, wine and mustard and microwave on HIGH for 2 minutes, stirring gently once during cooking.

3

Put the Béchamel sauce into a large cup and microwave on HIGH for 2 minutes or until thoroughly hot. Beat in half the cheeses and the yolk.

4

Pour into the lobster mixture and stir well. Cover with waxed paper and microwave on HIGH for 1 minute then continue on LOW if necessary, until the mixture is thoroughly hot.

5

Divide the mixture between the four lobster shell halves or put into individual flameproof dishes. Sprinkle with the remaining cheeses and brown under the grill.

Serves 4.

Note Crabmeat can be used in the same way.

Scampi Walewska

1 lb (450 g) shelled jumbo
shrimp, fresh or frozen
(uncooked)
3 Tbsp (45 ml) medium dry
sherry

For the sauce
2 Tbsp (25 g) butter or
margarine
2 Tbsp (25 g) all-purpose flour
$\frac{2}{3}$ cup (150 ml) milk
1 oz (25 g) Parmesan cheese,
grated
2 egg yolks
2 Tbsp (30 ml) light cream
$\frac{1}{4}$ level tsp (1.25 ml) salt
$\frac{1}{4}$ level tsp (1.25 ml) pepper

1

If using frozen shrimp, thaw it and
drain well on paper towels. Pat
dry.

2

Arrange the shrimp in an even
layer in a 9-inch (23-cm) shallow
dish, leaving a well in the middle.

3

Spoon the sherry evenly over the
shrimp. Cover with plastic wrap,
lifting up a corner to leave a tiny
gap. Microwave on HIGH for $3\frac{1}{2}$
minutes, giving the dish a quarter-
turn four times during cooking.
Leave covered while preparing
the sauce.

4

Put the butter in a medium bowl
and microwave on HIGH for 30
seconds or until melted.

5

Stir in the flour and microwave on
HIGH for 20 seconds or until the
mixture is puffy.

6

Stir in the milk and microwave on
HIGH for 2 minutes, whisking
frequently until the sauce thickens.

7

Measure the sauce and make up to
$1\frac{1}{4}$ cups (300 ml) with the juices
from the shrimp, adding extra milk
if necessary. Stir in the cheese.

8

Blend the egg yolks with the
cream, stir into the sauce and
season with the salt and pepper.
Microwave on HIGH for 45
seconds, whisking thoroughly
every 15 seconds.

9

Spread the shrimp out evenly in
the cooking dish or transfer to a
hot, microwave-suitable serving
dish. Pour over the sauce and
microwave on LOW for 2 minutes
or until reheated. Serve with
freshly boiled rice.

Serves 2–3.

Note This delightful sauce is
equally good with cooked scallops.

Smoked Salmon, Cucumber and Shrimp Toasts

$\frac{1}{2}$ cup (125 g) unsalted butter
5 Tbsp (75 ml) heavy cream
3 egg yolks, slightly beaten
2 Tbsp (30 ml) lemon juice
salt and freshly ground pepper
1 small cucumber, finely diced
and well drained
4 oz (125 g) cooked peeled
shrimp, thawed and well
drained
2 oz (50 g) smoked salmon, cut
into thin strips
8 slices brown or white bread
butter or margarine
paprika to garnish

1

Put the butter into a $1\frac{1}{2}$-pint
(900-ml) bowl and microwave on
HIGH for 1 minute or until melted.

2

Add the cream, egg yolks and
lemon juice and whisk until
smooth.

3

Reduce the setting and microwave
on LOW for 3 minutes or until the
sauce obviously thickens, whisking
every 30 seconds during cooking.
Continue beating for about 20
seconds, when it will thicken
further. Cover the surface with
plastic wrap and leave to cool.

4

Season to taste with salt and
pepper (do not add too much salt
as the salmon is salty). Stir in the
cucumber, shrimp and a third of
the smoked salmon.

5

Using a 3–4 inch (8–10 cm) cutter
or upturned glass, cut out a round
from each slice of bread.

6

Toast and lightly butter the bread
rounds and top with the shrimp
and cucumber mixture, arranging
remaining salmon strips on top.

Makes 8.

Trout with Almonds

¼ cup (50 g) butter or
   margarine
four 8 oz (225 g) trout, cleaned
salt and freshly ground pepper
½ cup (50 g) flaked almonds
lemon wedges, parsley or
   watercress sprigs to garnish

1

Preheat a browning dish according to the manufacturer's instructions, adding the butter for the last 30 seconds.

2

Meanwhile wipe the trout to dry them. Cut through the skin 3 times on each side. Rub in salt and pepper and set aside.

3

When the browning dish is hot and the butter brown and sizzling, quickly add the almonds; stir them around to color and coat with the butter. Remove the almonds on to paper towels using a slotted spoon.

4

Reheat the dish with the browned butter in it for 30 seconds. Turn the trout quickly in the butter to coat each side and microwave on HIGH for 3 minutes. Carefully turn the trout over, repositioning them, and microwave on HIGH for 4 minutes or until cooked.

5

Serve the trout with the almonds scattered over them and garnished with lemon wedges and parsley or watercress sprigs.

Serves 4.

Family Fish Pie

2 lb (900 g) white fish fillet,
   skinned, such as cod,
   haddock or hake
pinch of grated nutmeg
salt and freshly ground pepper
1½ lb (700 g) potatoes
2 Tbsp (25 g) butter or
   margarine
4 Tbsp (60 ml) milk

For the sauce
about 1¼ cups (300 ml) milk
3 Tbsp (40 g) butter or
   margarine
3 Tbsp (40 g) all-purpose flour
¼ level tsp (1.25 ml) prepared
   dry mustard
3 oz (75 g) Cheddar cheese,
   grated
salt and freshly ground pepper
paprika to garnish

1

Put the fish, 65 ml (2½ fl oz) water, nutmeg and salt into a casserole. Cover with cling film and microwave on HIGH for 7 minutes or until cooked.

2

Strain the liquid from the fish into a measure. Flake the fish, removing any bones.

3

Cook the potatoes (see page 77). When they are tender, strain them well and mash until smooth. Beat in the butter, milk, and salt and pepper to taste.

4

For the sauce, add milk to the fish liquid in the measure to make 450 ml (¾ pint). Make a basic white sauce (see page 91). When it is cooked stir in the mustard, cheese and the flaked fish. Add salt and pepper to taste.

5

Spread the fish in a 1½-quart (1.1-litre) baking dish and cover it with the potato, forking up the surface. Sprinkle paprika over the potato.

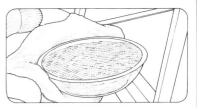

6

To reheat the pie, microwave on HIGH for 5 minutes or until hot.

Serves 4.

Note The pie freezes well. Individual pies are very useful.

CHAPTER FOUR

Meat

Meat is still the most popular main course and it is an excellent stand-by for snacks, quick burgers or suppers. Cooking by microwave is fast and clean, but meat is expensive and to get the best results it is worth studying the effect of microwave cooking on different cuts.

Meat does not tenderize well when cooked in the microwave oven, so always buy the best cuts that you can afford. Tougher cuts will be better if you tenderize the meat first by marinating, by sprinkling with meat tenderizing powder, by beating with a cleaver, or by chopping or mincing. On the whole, stew meats are not suitable for cooking in the microwave oven.

When fatty meats are microwaved, the melted fat is quickly drawn out and separates, settling in the cooking dish. This makes it an ideal way of cooking for dieters. Always remove the fat as it oozes out of the meat, as fat attracts the microwaves to itself, drawing them away from the meat. If much melted fat is left for long, spattering will occur.

Another factor governing how the meat cooks is the shape. Choose as even a shape as possible. Since microwaves cook more powerfully on the uppermost side of a large mass, turn the meat over halfway through cooking. Microwaves also have a greater cooking effect to a depth of about 1 inch (2.5 cm), so the inside of pieces thicker than this will cook more slowly than the outside.

Cooking times will vary with the size, shape and starting temperature of the meat, together with the tenderness factor and fat and water content. I have given my preferred power settings but there is no reason for you to adhere rigidly to these—for you may be in a hurry and wish to cook entirely on HIGH when speed is more important than tender results. Perhaps you have a lot of cooking to do and do not want to monopolize the oven with just one piece of meat. Not every oven has variable controls (a selection of power settings) and you may have to use a HIGH/LOW combination, instead of MEDIUM or MEDIUM HIGH and you will find advice on this in your manufacturer's handbook.

Microwave cooking is faster than conventional cooking but because there is no dry heat, some meats will not brown. These can be brushed with a colored sauce or condiment or be cooked in a dark-colored gravy.

Roasting

Choose even, compact shapes. They should have a thin layering of fat or you will find that the part near the thickest band of fat cooks too quickly. Larger pieces will brown because of the longer cooking time and a more pronounced browning can be obtained by raising the meat so that it is in the upper part of the oven. Small pieces can be brushed with a sauce or with brown or red colored spices.

Lean cuts can be roasted by any of the methods but fatty meat must be microwaved on a rack so that the melted fat can be removed easily during cooking.

Apart from the mini-roast, the best-textured piece of meat is that which is partially microwaved and finished in the conventional oven. However you will find that there is less shrinkage when meat is cooked entirely by microwave.

Roast Beef

If you like beef rare it is better to choose a cut of not more than 5 inches (12 cm) in diameter. Of course some of the family might prefer well-done meat, and the microwave oven copes well with this; simply microwave the meat on HIGH and reduce the cooking time correspondingly. The outside will be well done and the inside under done. Another way of cooking some parts rare and others well done is to buy a cut (without bone) and shape it thinner at one end—the thinner end will be the well-done one. A MEDIUM setting achieves more even cooking throughout the meat.

The mini-roast (see page 50), utilizing the browning dish, produces a specially succulent piece of meat and so it may be better to roast two of these consecutively than one large piece.

Beef Pot Roasts

Pot roasts can be cooked in the microwave oven but there is no substantial reduction in the cooking time compared with conventional cooking. If you have no other means of cooking, here is what you should do. Tenderize the meat before starting by marinating, rubbing with tenderizing powder or piercing deeply with a fork or skewer. Put the meat in a roasting bag in a shallow dish. Pour in no more than $\frac{2}{3}$ cup (150 ml) water and the flavoring vegetables and seasoning. Close the bag partially with a large elastic band or tie loosely with string, leaving a hole for the steam to escape. Microwave on LOW, carefully turning over the bag and meat halfway through cooking. Give the dish a quarter-turn three times during cooking. Allow about 45 minutes per 1 lb (450 g) beef. Leave the meat to stand for 20 minutes before removing from the bag.

Roast Lamb
The top half of a leg of lamb can be roasted in the same way as beef. Large pieces of lamb with the bone in cook successfully because the bone traps the heat; this causes the surrounding meat to cook more quickly, helping the meat in the center to catch up with the outsides. If there is no bone, pieces of smaller weights cook best.

When roasting the butt end, shield the bone with smoothed foil as soon as this part is cooked. (Make sure the foil does not touch the oven linings). A whole leg of lamb may be too long to fit into the microwave oven, so ask your butcher to partially snap the bone. Then you can fold it back and tie it to the upper part with string. Or buy a shank and butt end.

Shoulder of lamb should be roasted with the fatty side down for the first part of the cooking time, then turned.

A crown roast is an excellent microwave choice. Your butcher will prepare the meat for you if you don't wish to do it yourself. Stuff according to your favorite recipe and microwave on MEDIUM for 9–10 minutes per 1 lb (450 g). Shield the tips of the bones with foil and overwrap with plastic wrap. Allow a 20 minute standing time after cooking.

Roast Veal
Roast only rolled pieces as others cook unevenly. Veal contains very little fat and dries out quickly. Brush the veal with oil, then put in a roasting bag, adding a few cloves. Partially seal with an elastic band or string and put the bag in a shallow dish. Microwave on HIGH for the first 5 minutes, then reduce to LOW. Turn the bag and the veal over carefully halfway through cooking. A microwave thermometer or probe can be inserted through the bag into the joint—but make sure the dish can be turned if a probe is in position.

Roast Pork
This is the only piece of meat that should be salted before cooking. To obtain a crisper crackling, slash through the skin at 1-inch (2.5-cm) intervals and rub liberally with salt.

Steaks
Steak is so expensive that it really is better to cook them conventionally. The browning dish gives passable results but there is only a fractional saving of time on cooking and washing-up. Cook as for chops and follow the timings given on the chart (page 46). Strips and thin slices of fillet steak used in stir-fry and sauced speciality dishes are always well done and in these cases the browning dish is most satisfactory.

Chops
Choose chops $\frac{3}{4}$–1 inch (2–2.5 cm) thick and if more than one is being cooked, select chops of uniform weight and size.

Both lamb and pork chops can be cooked by microwave. Use the browning dish for lamb chops unless they are being sauced but pork chops can be cooked with or without the browning dish.

Ground Meats
Ground meats are the most versatile of meats. They are cheap, tender and can be easily divided into the quantities required. Freshly ground meat does not keep well and should be refrigerated or frozen after purchase. Frozen meat should be thawed before use.

Meat loaves, meat sauces, burgers and meat balls are all good stand-bys and hamburger can be made to go further when mixed with other ingredients such as breadcrumbs or rice.

Ground veal is leaner than lamb or beef. Par-cook fatty meats in a plastic colander over a large ovenproof glass bowl so that the melted fat can trickle through the holes and be drawn off. Stir the meat once during cooking and allow about 3 minutes per 1 lb (450 g) on HIGH. To fully brown ground meat allow 4 minutes. Chopped meat browns during a standing time if this is allowed. Remember when the fat has gone the weight of the meat will be correspondingly less, so that lean hamburger meat may be more economical. 1 lb (450 g) average ground beef weighs about 10 oz (275 g) after browning.

Meat loaf cooks quickly and uniformly on a HIGH setting if a ring mold is used. You can utilize a cake ring mold for this. Meat cooked in a ring mold will cook one-third quicker than in a loaf tin. Leave a standing time of 5–10 minutes after cooking.

When making long meat loaves you may find that the ends cook before the middle is ready. Shield these ends with foil as soon as they are cooked and continue microwaving until the center catches up. Cooking half the time on MEDIUM or HIGH and the remainder on LOW eliminates this problem. Always give the dishes a half-turn once during cooking, even when a turntable is used.

Meat Balls
Arrange meat balls in a circle in a round, square or oblong dish; turn them over and reposition two or three times during cooking. Giving the dish a turn occasionally also helps. Meat balls cooked without sauce will darken but not brown on the top. When cooking in a sauce, baste to keep them moist.

Variety Meats
Liver and kidneys are so well and quickly cooked in the microwave oven, that it would seem ludicrous to cook them any other way. Remove the sinewy vessels and inedible parts in the usual way and remove the skin if you can. If this proves too difficult, make sure the liver or kidneys are cut into slices or pieces. As long as these two popular meats are covered during cooking, splattering will be controlled. Do not be alarmed if you hear popping noises, as this is quite usual.

Sweetbreads must be soaked in cold salted water for at least 1 hour before cooking. Carefully cut out any tubes, fat and membrane to prevent damage to the sweetbreads. Then blanch them for 5 minutes in the microwave oven in a large bowl of salted boiling water acidulated with lemon juice. Drain, rinse in cold water and press out excess moisture with a clean dry cloth. Continue according to your favorite recipe.

Tongues cured by the butcher must be soaked for several hours. Immerse in plenty of boiling water in a covered casserole, adding herbs and seasoning. If the tongue is large, you will have to curve it. Allow 20 minutes per 1 lb (450 g) on HIGH or 50 minutes per 1 lb (450 g) on LOW. The LOW setting is better if you have time to spare.

Bacon

There are many ways of microwaving bacon, and it depends on how much trouble you wish to take, but the basic rule is to cover it in some way to prevent splatter-ing. Complete covering reduces the smells but the bacon will not be very crisp. A light covering with paper towels or waxed paper works well, but the paper must be removed immediately after cooking, otherwise the bacon sticks to the paper. Do not overcook bacon or it will become brittle.

When cooking several strips, overlap the fat and lean. Snip the rind if any before cooking, to prevent the bacon from curling. Microwave on HIGH allowing about 30 seconds per strip.

For 6 or more strips us a preheated browning dish or tray, putting a few fatty bacon trimmings in during the last minute or so of preheating. The melted fat acts as a coating to the dish or tray so that the bacon will not stick. When the dish is hot, arrange the bacon in a single layer and microwave on HIGH, turning the strips once during cooking.

For quantities between 8 oz and 1 lb (225 g and 450 g), overlap the slices on a rack over a shallow dish,

cover with waxed paper and microwave on HIGH for about 12 minutes per 1 lb (450 g), giving the dish a quarter-turn three times during cooking.

Fresh Ham

To keep the ham moist, remove the wrappings and cook in a roasting bag. Seal loosely with an elastic band or string and place the bag in a shallow dish. Microwave on HIGH for 5 minutes, turning the bag and ham over and reducing the setting to MEDIUM or LOW for the remaining cooking time (see the charts) when the thermometer should register 165° F/70° C. Tent loosely with foil and leave to stand for 10 minutes until the temperature reaches 170° C/75° C.

Cooked or Smoked Ham Roasts

These roasts require reheating only. Remove the wrapping and put the roast in a covered casserole, adding 1 Tbsp (15 ml) water, or in a roasting bag loosely secured with a large elastic band or string leaving a 1 inch (2.5 cm) gap. Place in a shallow dish.

Microwave on LOW giving the dish a half-turn halfway through the reheating period. Allow about 20 minutes per 1 lb (450 g). If using a meat thermometer to test the temperature it will read 130° F/55° C when the roast is ready. Leave in the covered casserole or the roasting bag for 10 minutes, during which time the temperature should rise to 140° F/60° C.

Sausages

Sausages can be cooked in the microwave oven but they will not brown or crisp unless the browning dish or tray is used. Prick the sausages thoroughly and reposition and turn them over during the cooking period.

An ordinary dish is a suitable utensil when the sausages are to be cut up after cooking for use in risottos or stews, but take care—the pallid color can belie the overcooked condition of the inside.

Use the microwave oven to take the chill off sausages and par-cook before frying or grilling conventionally. The browning dish will produce even crisper sausages if they are not refrigerator-cold when put into the preheated dish.

Cooking Meat

ROASTS	Per 1 lb (450 g): Rare on MEDIUM 11–13 minutes, on HIGH 6–7 minutes; Medium rare on MEDIUM 13–15 minutes, on HIGH 7–8 minutes; Well done on MEDIUM 15–17 minutes, on HIGH $8\frac{1}{2}$–9 minutes. Allow 15–20 minutes standing time.
STEAKS	1–2 minutes for 1 steak; 2–3 minutes for 3 steaks, depending on how rare they are to be served.
CHOPS **Lamb**	In pre-heated browning dish $1\frac{1}{2}$ minutes on HIGH, then further $1\frac{1}{2}$–2 minutes on MEDIUM.
Pork	Cook pork chops on HIGH. 1 average-sized chop will take 4–$4\frac{1}{2}$ minutes. 2 chops: 5–$5\frac{1}{2}$ minutes. 3 chops: 6–7 minutes. 4 chops: $6\frac{1}{2}$–8 minutes. Allow standing time of 2 minutes for 1 chop, 3–5 minutes for more. Much will depend on the shape of the chop.
STEW MEATS (Cubed)	Cooking time will entirely depend on quality and toughness of the meat, which should be cooked on as low a setting as possible.
VEAL **Cutlets**	2 minutes per cutlet on HIGH, depending on size.
Roast	Microwave on HIGH for 9 minutes per 1 lb (450 g) or 11 minutes on MEDIUM. Better results will be obtained if the first part of the cooking is carried out on HIGH, and the second period on MEDIUM.
POT ROAST	Microwave on LOW with $\frac{2}{3}$ cup (150 ml) water in roasting bag with vegetables and seasoning for 45 minutes per 1 lb (450 g). Allow 20 minutes standing time.
LIVER (Beef)	6–8 minutes per 1 lb (450 g) on HIGH.
SAUSAGES	2 sausages: $2\frac{1}{2}$ minutes in browning dish. 4 sausages: 4 minutes in browning dish.
BACON	1 strip: 30 seconds–1 minute on HIGH. 1 lb (450 g): 12–14 minutes on HIGH.

Thawing Meat

For frozen pieces of meat as well as whole roasts, the microwave is an ideal defroster. This enables you to choose your main course not more than an hour before the meal time. But, of course, if you do remember to get it out of the freezer the night before, dinner will be all the quicker.

Some meat dishes will be better cooked conventionally or partially by conventional means, but the recipes included in this chapter should satisfy the discerning eater. Although large roasts can be partially thawed on a MEDIUM setting I recommend thawing on LOW. This reduces the likelihood of the roasts cooking on the edges before thawing is complete. There is no absolute rule about unwrapping prior to thawing, but you will find it less messy if you are able to remove the Styrofoam tray if there is one. Roasts that are packaged completely in plastic wrap may be thawed initially without unwrapping but this should only be for long enough to enable you easily to peel away the wrapping. You should be able to do this after about one-quarter of the total thawing time.

Thawing Note In very round terms smaller pieces of any type of meat take between 6 and 10 minutes per 1 lb (450 g) followed by a standing time of about 10 minutes. Large pieces including roasts need a standing time halfway through thawing as well as after the indicated timing. Beefburgers take 16–20 minutes per 1 lb (450 g) to thaw.

	Thawing on LOW
BACON Package of sliced	One 8 oz (225 g) pack 2 minutes. Put the package in the microwave oven and microwave on LOW for 10 seconds. Turn over and microwave on LOW for a further 10 seconds. Leave to stand until the package can be flexed slightly, open and separate the strips. As soon as the slices can be separated the bacon is ready to cook. No standing time is necessary.
CHOPS Lamb	8–10 minutes. Separate during thawing and place bones to center. Shield if necessary. Turn over once. Allow to stand for 5–10 minutes.
Pork	As for lamb.
STEW MEATS (Cubed)	6–8 minutes per 1 lb (450 g). Stir three times. Standing time 10–15 minutes.
ROASTS	Total microwave time 7–10 minutes per 1 lb (450 g). It is best to thaw for 3 minutes,, then turn over and thaw for further 3 minutes, rest for 10 minutes, continue microwaving on LOW for 3 minutes, give a further 20 minutes rest, then continue microwaving for a last 2 minutes per 1 lb (450 g) with a final 2 minutes per 1 lb (450 g) resting time.
LIVER (Beef)	8–10 minutes per 1 lb (450 g). Separate during thawing. Leave to stand for 5 minutes.
SAUSAGES	4–6 minutes 1 lb (450 g).
STEAKS	As for chops. Reposition sides to middle during thawing.
VEAL Cutlets	As for chops. Take great care to shield warmed parts.
Roast	As for roasts above.

Thawing Large Roasts

1

Put the packaged roast, Styrofoam tray underneath, in a large shallow dish. Microwave on LOW for the first period (see chart).

2

Remove the tray and wrappings. Put an upturned, undecorated saucer or rack in the dish.

3

Turn the roast over and put on the saucer or rack and microwave on LOW for the second period.

4

Shield with small pieces of smooth foil any parts of the joint that seem warm to the touch.

5

Without altering the position of the shielding foil, turn the roast over and allow a 10 minute standing time. Mop up any juices with paper towels.

6

Microwave on LOW for a third period, shielding warm parts with foil as before. Continue to mop up any juices with paper towels.

7

Turn the roast over and leave to stand for 20 minutes, then remove the foil.

8

Insert a skewer into the roast. Under firm pressure it should pass all the way through if the joint is completely thawed. Allow a standing time equal to the thawing time.

Thawing Chops and Steaks

1

Remove from the package and put on a rack over a shallow dish. Single chops or steaks can be thawed on an upturned undecorated saucer.

2

Microwave on LOW, separating the pieces as soon as possible. Arrange the meat thicker parts toward the outside.

3

Shield the edges with small, smooth pieces of foil, making sure that the foil cannot touch the oven lining.

4

Turn the meat over, reposition and shield where necessary. To test whether the meat is thawed, frequently press the surface of the meat with the fingers.

5

Remove the pieces when they are cold but not icy to the touch and a skewer inserted through the top surface can be pushed through to the underside. Leave to stand for 5–10 minutes to complete thawing.

Mini Roast (page 50)

Thawing Stew Meat (Cubed)

1

Put the package in a dish in the microwave oven and microwave on LOW long enough to enable you to unwrap the package.

2

Spread the unwrapped meat in a large shallow baking dish and microwave on LOW for as long as it takes for the surface of the meat to give to the touch. Stir three times during this period, pushing the frozen pieces to the outside.

3

Using paper towels, mop up any liquid which oozes out or pour it off if you wish to save it for use in sauces, gravies or stews.

4

Leave to stand for 10–15 minutes or until a piece can be speared with a fork. If the meat is to be cooked by microwave, prick all pieces thoroughly to help to tenderize.

Lamb, Eggplant and Red Pepper Kebabs (page 53)

Thawing Ground Meats

1

To thaw an entire package:
Put the wrapped package on the oven shelf and microwave on LOW until the top surface softens. Turn the package over and microwave on LOW until the upper surface softens again.

2

Remove the wrappings, scrape off the thawed parts and put them in a dish. Turn the frozen section into another dish and microwave on LOW, breaking up the pieces and stirring as it becomes possible.

3

As soon as any parts soften remove them from the dish. Leave to stand for 5–10 minutes until the lumps can be flattened with a fork.

Note If the frozen meat you are using is not the quantity needed for your recipe, thaw on the lowest microwave setting and break away the semi-thawed parts for immediate use, returning the rest to the freezer immediately.
   Thin burgers can be cooked from frozen. Burgers over $\frac{1}{4}$ inch (0.5 cm) thick should be thawed on the lowest setting. Arrange in a circle on the oven shelf or a plate and turn over and reposition frequently.

Meat Gravy

**cooking juices from the roast beef stock
1 level Tbsp (15 ml) cornstarch
gravy browning, optional
salt and freshly ground pepper**

1

Collect the meat cooking juices from the joint and pour into a large measuring cup. Remove any fat.

2

Make up to $2\frac{1}{4}$ cups (450 ml) with beef stock. Microwave on HIGH for 3 minutes or until boiling.

3

Blend the cornstarch with a little water and stir into the stock.

4

Microwave on HIGH for 3 minutes until the gravy thickens. Stir once during cooking. Add a few drops of gravy browning for a darker color if wished. Season to taste.

Serves 6.

Note If you prefer a slightly thicker gravy add an extra 1 level tsp (5 ml) cornstarch.

Mini-Roast

2-lb (900-g) rolled roast of beef
6–7 inches (15–18 cm) across
vegetable oil
Meat Gravy (page 49)

1

Cut the roast in half lengthwise, then re-shape each piece to a small roast not more than 7.5 cm (3 inches) in diameter.

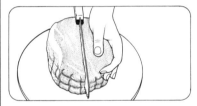

2

Tie with string at ½-inch (1-cm) intervals. Cook the roasts one at a time. Each roast will serve three. Brush the ends of the roasts with oil. Heat a browning dish to maximum according to the manufacturer's instruction booklet.

3

Using tongs quickly put the beef, end up, into the dish and seal the end. Turn it and seal the other end.

4

Lay the roast on its fatty side (only one side of the beef will have a covering of fat due to the way it has been divided) and seal. Quickly turn the beef to seal the leaner side. Then microwave on HIGH for 4 minutes, turning the roast over halfway through cooking.

5

Transfer to a heated serving dish, tent with foil and leave to stand for 3 minutes before carving.

6

Meanwhile wipe out the browning dish and reheat for 3 minutes, then cook the second roast. Serve with gravy and vegetables of your choice.

Serves 6.

Note A microwaved mini-roast is roast beef at its best since there is no chance of some parts being overcooked while others are rare. 4 minutes cooking gives a rare roast; for medium rare, microwave for up to 5 minutes. Further cooking will cause the outer edge to be overdone.

Chops in the Browning Dish

pork loin or rib chops, or lamb
chops, trimmed
oil, salted butter or margarine
salt and freshly ground black
pepper

1

Dab the chops with paper towels to remove excess moisture.

2

Brush all surfaces with oil, salted butter or margarine. Preheat the browning dish or tray to the maximum recommended by the manufacturer.

3

Quickly press the chops on to the hot surface, bone ends toward the middle. Microwave on HIGH for 1 minute, then immediately turn the chops over keeping the bone ends toward the middle.

4

For lamb chops reduce the setting to MEDIUM and continue cooking. Complete cooking pork chops on HIGH. Give the dish a half-turn once during cooking.

5

Test with the tip of a sharp knife. With lamb, the juices should run clear and the flesh should be opaque. Pork should not have any pink color showing inside.

6

Leave to stand for 3–5 minutes before serving. Season to taste and serve on heated plates.

Steaks in the Browning Dish

good-quality lean beef steak
2 Tbsp (25 g) butter or
  margarine
parsley butter to garnish

1

Feel the steaks and if they are cold to the touch put them on a plate and microwave on LOW for 1 minute just to take off the chill.

2

To seal steaks in the microwave oven, preheat the browning dish to maximum according to the manufacturer's instructions. Add the butter or margarine during the last 30 seconds. When the butter is dark brown add the steaks, pressing them flat with a fish slice.

3

Immediately turn the steaks over and microwave on HIGH for 1 minute. Cook the steaks according to personal taste (see chart on page 46), giving the dish a half-turn after a further minute. Serve garnished with parsley butter.

Cubed steak

Tender cuts of beef, lamb and pork are all suitable for microwave cooking. They can be browned first in a browning dish, used in stir-fry recipes, for kebabs or served with a sauce.

Beef Stroganoff

$1\frac{1}{4}$ lb (550 g) fillet steak, cut in
  thin strips
$1\frac{1}{3}$ cups (75 g) butter or
  margarine
1 large onion, peeled and finely
  chopped
6 oz (175 g) button mushrooms,
  wiped and finely sliced
1 level Tbsp (15 ml) all-purpose
  flour
$\frac{2}{3}$ cup (150 ml) sour cream
salt and freshly ground pepper

1

Preheat a browning dish according to the manufacturer's instructions, adding 2 Tbsp (25 g) butter during the last 20 seconds.

2

When the butter is brown and without removing the dish from the oven, add half the steak strips, turning and pressing them flat against the surface with a spatula.

3

Microwave on HIGH for 30 seconds or until sealed all over. Remove the meat and set aside.

4

Carefully wipe out the hot browning dish with a thick wad of paper towels and heat it again for 2 minutes, adding $\frac{1}{2}$ Tbsp (7 g) butter toward the end. Seal the remaining meat as before. Remove and set aside with the other steak strips.

5

Using the same dish or another suitable casserole, combine the remaining $\frac{1}{4}$ cup (50 g) butter with the onion. Stir well, partially cover with plastic wrap and microwave on HIGH for 3 minutes. Mix in the sliced mushrooms and microwave for 1 minute or until the onion and mushrooms are soft.

6

Stir in the flour and microwave on HIGH for 1 minute, stirring briskly two or three times during cooking.

7

Beat in the sour cream, any juices from the meat and salt and pepper to taste. Cover and microwave on HIGH for 1 minute or until hot. Stir occasionally during cooking.

8

Stir all the strips of steak into the sauce, then cover and microwave on HIGH for 2 minutes or until the meat is reheated and cooked to taste. Stir once during reheating, paying particular attention to the sauce around the edges. Serve with boiled potatoes or rice, spinach or broccoli and carrots if you wish.

Serves 4–6.

Note The sauce can also be used for coating whole or sliced steaks that have been completely cooked in the conventional way. The sauce is sufficient for coating 6–8 steaks.

Italian Meat Balls

2 slices dry bread, crusts
  removed
1 lb (450 g) lean beef, freshly
  ground
1 small onion, peeled and
  minced
½ clove garlic, peeled and
  crushed
1 oz (25 g) Cheddar cheese,
  grated
2 Tbsp (30 ml) chopped parsley
2 eggs
salt and freshly ground pepper
8 oz (225 g) tagliatelle
1 tsp (5 ml) vegetable oil

For the sauce
1 medium onion, peeled and
  finely chopped
3 bacon rinds or chunks
2 Tbsp (25 g) all-purpose flour
1¼ cups (300 ml) tomato juice
1 beef bouillon cube, crumbled
1 bay leaf, crumbled
½ level tsp (2.5 ml) sugar
salt and freshly ground pepper

1

Soak the bread in cold water for 5 minutes, then squeeze dry and mash in a large bowl.

2

Add the ground beef, onion, garlic, cheese, parsley and eggs and season to taste. Knead the ingredients until well blended.

3

Divide the mixture into sixteen and shape into 1½-inch (4-cm) balls (they will be very soft).

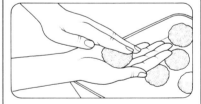

4

Arrange in a single layer in a shallow dish and, without covering, microwave on HIGH for 5 minutes or until half cooked. Give the dish a quarter-turn three times during this period.

5

Drain away any fat that may have gathered in the dish. Cover the meat balls and set aside while making the sauce.

6

To make the sauce, put the onion and bacon rinds in a medium bowl and microwave on HIGH for 2 minutes or until the onion is soft. Stir in the flour and microwave on HIGH for 1 minute, stirring after 30 seconds. Add the tomato juice, beef cube, bay leaf and sugar and microwave on HIGH for 2 minutes. Stir in ⅔ cup (150 ml) hot water and microwave on HIGH for 3 minutes until the sauce thickens. Add salt and pepper to taste.

7

Reposition the meat balls, taking care that they do not break as they are very soft, and strain the sauce over the meat. Microwave on HIGH for 3 minutes or until the meat balls are fully cooked. Cover.

8

Prepare the pasta. See Cooking Noodles (page 85). Drain the pasta and arrange in a border around the meat. Serve with zucchini and mushrooms, if you wish.

Serves 4–6.

Chili con Carne

1 lb (450 g) lean ground beef
1 medium onion, peeled and
  finely chopped
1 green pepper, seeded and
  finely chopped
14-oz (396-g) can tomatoes,
  with their juice
14-oz (396-g) can kidney beans,
  drained
5-oz (142-ml) can tomato paste
2 level tsp (10 ml) chili powder
½ level tsp (2.5 ml) ground
  cumin
½ level tsp (2.5 ml) salt
¼ level tsp (1.25 ml) pepper

1

Mix the beef, onion and green pepper in a large casserole. Stir thoroughly, cover and microwave on HIGH for 8 minutes or until the meat changes color. Stir twice during cooking, making sure that the beef pieces are well broken up.

2

Add all the remaining ingredients and ½ cup (125 ml) water. Stir. Cover and microwave on HIGH for 10 minutes, then reduce the setting and microwave on LOW for 1 hour. Stir occasionally during cooking. Serve with garlic bread or toast and a green salad.

Serves 6–8.

Note Half this quantity will take about 40 minutes in all. Chili con carne can be cooked entirely on a HIGH setting: when all ingredients have been added microwave on HIGH for 25 minutes. This method is perfectly suitable if the Chili con carne can be prepared 24 hours in advance. To reheat, cover and microwave on HIGH for 5 minutes or until thoroughly hot. Stir occasionally during reheating.

Beefburgers

1 lb (450 g) beef, freshly ground
small piece of onion, peeled
   and grated
1 egg
few drops of Worcestershire
   sauce
1 level tsp (5 ml) salt
freshly ground pepper
$\frac{1}{2}$ level tsp (2.5 ml) mixed dried
   herbs
1 Tbsp (15 g) butter

1

Mix all ingredients except the
butter thoroughly together. Shape
into four burgers.

2

Preheat a large browning dish to
maximum according to the
manufacturer's instructions,
adding the butter during the last
30 seconds.

3

Immediately press the beefburgers
flat on to the hot surface and
microwave on HIGH for 5 minutes
or until just cooked, turning the
burgers over and repositioning
after 3 minutes. Serve with Quick
Tomato Sauce (see page 93),
mashed potato and shredded
cabbage if you wish. Or serve in
burger buns topped with pickles,
onion rings and tomato on lettuce-
lined plates.

Serves 4.

Note The burgers can be covered
for the last 2 minutes if preferred.
Reduce the cooking time to just
over 3 minutes for 2 burgers or $1\frac{3}{4}$
minutes for 1 burger.

Lamb, Eggplant and Red Pepper Kebabs

2 lb (900 g) boned leg of lamb,
   trimmed and cut into $\frac{3}{4}$-inch
   (2-cm) cubes
2 medium eggplant, halved
   lengthwise and cut into
   $\frac{3}{4}$-inch (2-cm) slices
2 red peppers, seeded and cut
   into $1\frac{1}{2}$-inch (4-cm) pieces
2 small onions, peeled and cut
   into 8 wedges

For the marinade
2 Tbsp (25 g) butter
1 small onion, peeled and finely
   chopped
$\frac{1}{2}$ green pepper, seeded and
   finely chopped
1 celery stalk, finely chopped
1 clove garlic, crushed
8-oz (226-g) can tomatoes
8 level Tbsp (120 ml) tomato
   paste
2 level Tbsp (30 ml) dark brown
   sugar
$1\frac{1}{2}$ tsp (7.5 ml) lemon juice
$\frac{1}{2}$ level tsp (2.5 ml) salt
$\frac{1}{2}$ tsp (2.5 ml) Tabasco

1

Make the marinade. Put the butter,
onion, green pepper, celery and
garlic into a large bowl, cover and
microwave on HIGH for 8 minutes,
stirring occasionally.

2

Add all the remaining marinade
ingredients plus 75 ml (5 tbsp)
water and microwave on HIGH for
5 minutes or until boiling. Reduce
the setting and microwave on LOW
for 10 minutes. Leave to cool. The
marinade should be of a thick sauce
consistency. Add another 30–45 ml
(2–3 tbsp) water if you prefer.

3

Stir in the lamb and mix well.
Cover and chill for at least 4 hours.

4

Put the aubergines, red peppers
and onion wedges into a bowl, add
30 ml (2 tbsp) water, cover and
microwave on HIGH for 3 minutes
or until the vegetables are slightly
soft. Drain. Cover and set aside
until the lamb is ready to cook.

5

Thread the lamb, eggplant,
pepper and onion pieces onto
wooden skewers.

6

Arrange in a double layer on a
roasting rack in a shallow dish.
Microwave on HIGH for 6 minutes,
then reposition so that the inside
kebabs are moved to the outside of
the dish. Spoon the marinade over
the kebabs and microwave on
HIGH for 15 minutes or until the
lamb is cooked. Reposition the
kebabs twice during this cooking
period. Transfer to a hot dish.

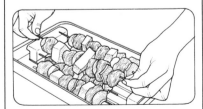

7

The thin sauce which you will find
in the bottom of the dish can be
reheated and served separately.

Serves 4–6.

Lamb and Artichoke Gratin

1½ lb (700 g) lean lamb, freshly
    ground
salt and freshly ground pepper
juice of 1 lime
4 level tsp (20 ml) all-purpose
    flour
4 Tbsp (60 ml) dry white wine
14-oz (397-g) can artichoke
    hearts, drained
1 level Tbsp (15 ml) grated
    Parmesan cheese
2 level Tbsp (30 ml) fresh
    breadcrumbs

1

Spread the meat out in a 9-inch
(23-cm) round shallow ovenproof
glass dish, season with salt and
pepper and sprinkle with the lime
juice. Leave for 2 hours. Microwave
on HIGH for 10 minutes or until
the meat is just cooked. Stir and
break up the lumps two or three
times during cooking.

2

Mix the flour and wine together
and pour over the meat. Stir
thoroughly and microwave on
HIGH for 2 minutes or until the
mixture thickens slightly.

3

Chop the artichokes and spread
over the meat. Sprinkle with the
Parmesan cheese and the
breadcrumbs, preferably mixed
together. Microwave on HIGH for
2 minutes, then give the dish a half-
turn and microwave on HIGH for a
further 2 minutes or until the
artichokes are hot. Brown under
the grill.

Serves 4.

Lamb Chops Paprika

four 6-oz (175-g) lamb chops,
    trimmed
2 level Tbsp (30 ml) flour
    seasoned with paprika
1 Tbsp (15 g) butter or
    margarine
1 red pepper, seeded and cut
    into rings
1 medium onion, peeled and
    finely sliced
1 level Tbsp (15 ml) paprika
salt and freshly ground pepper
⅔ cup (150 ml) heavy cream

1

Coat the chops lightly in seasoned
flour. Preheat the browning dish to
maximum according to
manufacturer's instructions,
adding the butter during the last
15 seconds.

2

Quickly put the chops into the
sizzling butter and turn them over.
Microwave on HIGH for 3 minutes.
Turn the chops over and
reposition, then add the red
pepper and onion. Cover and
microwave on HIGH for 6 minutes,
repositioning the chops once.

3

Sprinkle the chops with the
paprika, salt and pepper and
microwave on HIGH for 2 minutes.

4

Stir in the cream round the sides of
the dish and, without covering,
microwave on HIGH for 2 minutes
until the sauce is hot. Stir once.

Serves 4.

Note If browning is not
important, cook in a casserole.

Pork Fillet with Cashew Nuts

2 Tbsp (25 g) butter or
    margarine
1 lb (450 g) pork cutlet
    (boneless), thinly sliced
4 stalks of celery, trimmed and
    thinly sliced
grated rind and juice of 1
    orange
⅔ cup (150 ml) chicken stock
salt and freshly ground pepper
1 level Tbsp (15 ml) cornstarch
2 oz (50 g) cashew nuts

1

Preheat the browning dish to
maximum according to the
manufacturer's instructions,
adding the butter for the
last 30 seconds, without removing
the dish from the oven.

2

Immediately add the pork slices
and stir quickly. Microwave on
HIGH for 2 minutes. Add the
celery slices and stir. Microwave on
HIGH for a further 2 minutes.

3

Add the orange rind and juice,
stock and seasoning and cook for
2 minutes on HIGH. Blend the
cornstarch to a paste with a little
water and stir into the juices. Add
the cashew nuts and microwave on
HIGH for 2 minutes or until the
juices have thickened. Serve with
rice and a crisp side salad.

Serves 4.

Pork Chop on a Plate

8-oz (225-g) pork chop
vegetable oil

1

Trim away excess fat and brush one side of the chop with vegetable oil.

2

Put the chop oily side down on a plate and cover with waxed paper to prevent splattering.

3

Microwave on HIGH for 2 minutes or until cooked. Test with the point of a sharp knife.

4

Season to taste and leave for 2 minutes before serving with apple sauce, a baked potato and green beans if you wish.

Serves 1.

Note Trimming will probably remove 1½ oz (40 g) from the original weight. Cooking times are variable, depending on size of chop, amount of fat, and so on.

Granny's Pork Chops in Cider

3 Tbsp (40 g) butter or
  margarine
four 6-oz (175-g) pork chops,
  trimmed
salt and freshly ground pepper
3 level Tbsp (45 ml) all-purpose
  flour
3 green apples, each peeled,
  cored and cut into 8 wedges
1 cup (240 ml) dry or extra dry
  cider

1

Preheat a large browning dish according to the manufacturer's instructions adding the butter in 2 pieces during the last 30 seconds.

2

Meanwhile season the chops and coat with flour. Reserve the remaining flour. When the browning dish is hot and the butter dark brown and sizzling, quickly add the chops, pressing them down with a spatula.

3

Turn the chops over quickly to seal the other side. Microwave on HIGH for 5 minutes, repositioning and turning the chops over halfway through cooking. Remove the chops and set aside.

4

Stir the prepared apples into the butter left in the dish. Cover and microwave on HIGH for 3 minutes or until the apples are tender. Stir once during cooking. Stir in the remaining flour and mix in the cider.

5

Arrange the chops on top of the apples, browner side down. Cover with the lid and microwave on HIGH for 8 minutes or until the chops are cooked. Turn the chops over and reposition halfway through the cooking time.

6

Serve the chops browner side up, garnished with a few pieces of apple, and pour the sauce over. Serve with salad or green beans, if you wish.

Serves 4.

Note To cook the chops without the browning dish, pre-cook the chops on HIGH for 5 minutes without additional fat. Remove from the dish while melting the butter and cooking the apples.

Pork Chops with Red Currant Glaze

4 pork chops, $\frac{3}{4}$-1 inch
  (2–2.5 cm) thick
1 Tbsp (15 g) butter or
  margarine
salt and freshly ground pepper
4 Tbsp (60 ml) red currant jelly
1 Tbsp (15 ml) red wine vinegar
$\frac{1}{2}$ level tsp (2.5 ml) Dijon-style
  mustard

1

Trim any excess fat from the chops and pat dry to remove any excess moisture. Preheat the browning dish to maximum according to manufacturer's instructions, adding the butter for the last 30 seconds.

2

Without removing the browning dish from the oven, quickly press the chops on to the hot surface, placing the bony ends toward the center of the dish. Microwave on HIGH for 3 minutes, then turn the chops over and reposition.

3

Continue to microwave on HIGH for 6 minutes or until the chops are tender—and until there is no trace of pink inside. Give the dish a half turn once during cooking. Leave to stand, covered, for 5 minutes before serving. Season to taste.

4

Meanwhile put the red currant jelly, vinegar and mustard in a large measuring cup, stir and microwave on HIGH for $3\frac{1}{2}$ minutes or until syrupy. Pour the glaze over the chops and serve.

Serves 4.

Veal Scallops in Onion and Cream Sauce

4 veal scallops, each about 4 oz
  (100 g)
salt and freshly ground pepper
2 Tbsp (25 g) butter or
  margarine

For the sauce
1 medium onion, peeled and
  finely chopped
2 Tbsp (25 g) butter or
  margarine
6 Tbsp (90 ml) dry white wine
$\frac{2}{3}$ cup (150 ml) heavy cream
salt
$\frac{1}{4}$ tsp (1.25 ml) lemon juice

1

Flatten the veal cutlets to $\frac{1}{8}$ inch (0.25 cm) thick. Dry with paper towels, and season.

2

Put the butter in a large shallow dish, cover lightly and microwave on HIGH for 3 minutes or until foaming.

3

Quickly remove the covering, add the scallops and microwave on HIGH for 2 minutes. Turn over and reposition the scallops and microwave on HIGH for $1\frac{1}{2}$ minutes or until just cooked. Drain, then cover and set aside.

4

Make the sauce. Put the onion and butter in another dish. Microwave on HIGH for 2 minutes or until the onion is soft, stirring once during cooking.

5

Stir in the wine and microwave on HIGH for 1 minute or until boiling.

6

Add the cream, salt to taste and microwave on HIGH for 2 minutes or until boiling, stirring twice during cooking. Allow to cool slightly, then purée the sauce in a blender and stir in the lemon juice.

7

Pour the sauce over the veal. Without covering, microwave on LOW for 2 minutes or until reheated. Take care not to overheat the sauce or it will curdle. Serve with rice or new potatoes and green beans or spinach, if you wish.

Serves 4.

Note The veal can be sealed first in a frying pan if preferred. If 4 scallops are too large to make a single layer in the dish, cook 2 at a time. Add half the butter for the first 2, add the remaining butter and microwave until foaming. Reheat all the scallops in the sauce.

Sautéed Veal or Pork Scallops

4 veal or pork scallops, each
   about 4 oz (100 g), trimmed
   and flattened
2 Tbsp (25 g) butter or
   margarine
2 Tbsp (30 ml) brandy

1

Heat the butter or margarine in
a shallow dish on HIGH for
3 minutes or until foaming.

2

Add the scallops and microwave
on HIGH for 2 minutes. Turn over,
reposition the scallops and
microwave on HIGH for 1½
minutes or until cooked.

3

Put the brandy in a glass and warm
in the microwave on HIGH for
5 seconds, then pour over the veal
in the dish and flambé. While the
flames are leaping, swirl the
scallops round in the sauce.

Serves 4.

Note Scallops can also be cooked
by dipping in beaten egg and
golden crumbs. Microwave in
1 Tbsp (15 ml) oil. Turn the scallops
over halfway through cooking.

Kidneys or Chicken Livers in Madeira

8 lambs' kidneys, about 1 lb
   (450 g), or 1 lb (450 g) chicken
   livers
2 Tbsp (30 ml) Madeira
2 Tbsp (25 g) butter or
   margarine
1 clove garlic, peeled and
   crushed
1 Tbsp (15 ml) chopped fresh
   parsley
½ tsp (2.5 ml) Worcestershire
   sauce
½ level tsp (2.5 ml) dry mustard
1 level tsp (5 ml) cornstarch

For micro-fried crumbs
¼ cup (50 g) butter or
   margarine
½ cup (50 g) fresh breadcrumbs

1

Skin the kidneys and cut in half
horizontally. Remove the core
with scissors or a sharp knife. If
using chicken livers, cut larger
livers in half.

2

Put the kidneys or livers into a
small bowl, add the Madeira and
stir well. Leave to stand for 15
minutes, stirring occasionally.

3

Put the butter in a casserole and
microwave on HIGH for 5 seconds
or until very soft but not melted.
Mix the garlic, parsley,
Worcestershire sauce and mustard
powder into the butter.

4

Drain the kidneys or livers,
reserving the Madeira juices, and
stir into the flavored butter,
turning the pieces so that they are
well coated. Cover and microwave
on HIGH for 4½ minutes or until
cooked (do not overcook). Stir,
turn over and rearrange the pieces
twice during cooking.

5

Remove the kidneys or livers to a
warm serving dish with a slotted
spoon.

6

Stir the cornstarch into the
reserved Madeira and pour into
the meat juices in the casserole
(there is no need to cover the
dish). Microwave on HIGH for 1
minute or until the sauce thickens,
stirring once during cooking. Pour
the sauce over the kidneys or
livers.

7

To prepare the fried crumbs put
the butter into a shallow dish and
microwave on HIGH for 1 minute
or until foaming.

8

Sprinkle the breadcrumbs evenly
over the surface, then stir and
microwave on HIGH for 1 minute.
Stir once more, then microwave
on HIGH for 2–2½ minutes or until
the butter is absorbed and the
breadcrumbs are slightly colored.

9

To serve, put the crumbs into a
small dish and hand round
separately. Serve with Soft Sautéed
Potatoes (see page 82) and green
beans, if you wish.

Serves 4.

Note The micro-fried crumbs can
be prepared in advance and
reheated for a few seconds just
before serving.

Liver and Onions

4–6 strips bacon, without rind
1 lb (450 g) calves liver, thinly
   sliced
2 Tbsp (25 g) butter or
   margarine
2 medium onions, peeled and
   chopped
2 level Tbsp (30 ml) fresh
   breadcrumbs (optional)
$\frac{2}{3}$ cup (150 ml) hot beef stock
1 bay leaf

1

Cook the bacon as instructed on
page 46 and set aside.

2

Wash the liver in cold water and
cut out any inedible membranes.
Pat dry on paper towels.

3

Put the butter or margarine in a
flameproof casserole and
microwave on HIGH for 45 seconds
or until melted.

4

Stir in the onions and microwave
on HIGH for 3 minutes until the
onions are soft, stirring once
during cooking.

5

Add the liver and turn the pieces
to coat with the onion mixture.
Sprinkle with the breadcrumbs, if
wished. Pour over the stock, add
the bayleaf and lay the bacon on
top.

6

Cover and microwave on HIGH for
3 minutes. Reposition the liver,
recover and microwave on HIGH
for 3$\frac{1}{2}$ minutes or until tender.
Brown under the grill, if wished.

Serves 4.

Ham Steaks

4-oz (125-g) ham steak
2 tsp (10 ml) honey
$\frac{1}{4}$ level tsp (1.25 ml) Dijon-style
   mustard

1

Remove the rind and snip around
the edges at $\frac{1}{2}$-inch (1-cm)
intervals to prevent the steak
curling. Put on a dish or plate and
cover with waxed paper.

2

Microwave on HIGH for 2 minutes.
Brush with honey and mustard and
cook for a further 30 seconds or
until just cooked. Do not
overcook. Leave to stand for 3
minutes during which time the
ham will finish cooking. Ham
steaks tend to "pop" during
cooking.

3

Transfer to a warm plate and
garnish with pineapple, peaches,
mandarin segments or apple rings.

Serves 1.

Note A 6-oz (175-g) ham steak will
take 2$\frac{1}{2}$–3 minutes. Two steaks will
take approximately 4$\frac{1}{2}$ minutes. If
cooking more than 1 steak at the
same time, give the dish a quarter-
turn three times during cooking
even if your oven is fitted with a
turntable.

Sausages in the Browning Dish

4 large pork or beef sausages
prepared mustard or prepared
   sauce to serve

1

First put the sausages on a plate
and microwave on LOW for 10
seconds or until they are no longer
cold to the touch. To take the chill
off a pack of 4 (not frozen) sausages,
leave in the wrapping and turn the
package over after 5 seconds.
Remove the wrapping and separate
the sausages. Prick them
thoroughly.

2

Preheat a large browning dish to
the maximum recommended by
the manufacturer, adding a small
dab of butter or margarine during
the last 30 seconds.

3

Put the sausages in the dish,
moving them quickly around with
tongs. Microwave on HIGH, for 3
minutes or until cooked,
repositioning and turning the
sausages over once during cooking.
Serve with mustard or sauce, if
wished.

Note If more than 4 large
sausages are being cooked, it is
better to drain the fat from the
browning dish and reheat for 2
minutes before cooking another
batch. There will be no need to add
any extra fat.

Sausage and Bacon Rolls

12 strips bacon
12 oz (350 g) sausage meat

1

Remove the rind, if still on, and stretch the bacon with the back of a knife.

2

Divide the sausage meat into 12 even portions and shape into small rolls.

3

Place a sausage roll on one end of each strip of bacon and roll up so that the bacon is coiled around the sausage leaving no gap.

4

Arrange in a shallow dish seam sides underneath and microwave on HIGH for 10 minutes or until the sausage meat is cooked. Reposition the bacon rolls twice during cooking, making sure that those in the center are pushed to the outside and vice versa. Drain on paper towel. Brown under a hot grill if wished.

Serves 4.

Tomato Meat Loaf with Rich Brown Sauce

$1\frac{1}{4}$ lb (550 g) lean beef, freshly ground
1 medium onion, peeled and finely chopped
2 oz (50 g) fresh breadcrumbs
14-oz (396-g) can tomatoes, well drained
1 egg, beaten
2 level tsp (10 ml) salt
$\frac{1}{2}$ level tsp (2.5 ml) black pepper
$\frac{1}{2}$ level tsp (2.5 ml) dried basil
$\frac{1}{4}$ tsp (1.25 ml) Worcestershire sauce
$\frac{2}{3}$ cup (150 ml) Rich Brown Sauce (see page 95)

1

Combine all the ingredients except the rich brown sauce in a mixing bowl. Mix well.

2

Press the mixture evenly into a 1-quart (1-l) ring mold.

3

Microwave on HIGH for 10 minutes or until the inside edge of the meat is just cooked. Give the dish a quarter-turn four times during cooking. Turn out on to a hot serving dish.

4

Put the sauce in a sauceboat or measuring cup and microwave on HIGH for 1 minute or until heated, stirring occasionally. Pour the sauce over the meat and serve at once.

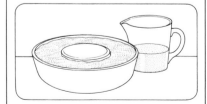

Serves 6–8.

Sausages with Green Beans

8 large pork sausages, pricked
2 Tbsp (25 g) butter or margarine
1 large onion, peeled and thinly sliced
8 oz (225 g) French beans, trimmed and cut into 2-inch (5-cm) pieces
$\frac{2}{3}$ cup (150 ml) beef stock
1 level Tbsp (15 ml) mild prepared mustard
salt and freshly ground pepper

1

Preheat a browning dish to maximum according to the manufacturer's instructions, adding 1 Tbsp (15 g) of the butter for the last 30 seconds.

2

Without removing the browning dish from the oven, quickly put 4 of the sausages on to the hot surface and move them around quickly using a pair of tongs. Microwave on HIGH for 1 minute, then remove the sausages and set aside.

3

Drain the fat from the browning dish and reheat on HIGH for 2 minutes. Add the remaining sausages turning on the hot surface and moving them around quickly. Microwave on HIGH for 1 minute, then remove the sausages and set aside.

4

Add the remaining butter to the browning dish with the onion and beans and microwave on HIGH for 2 minutes. Return the sausages to the dish, add the stock, mustard and seasoning. Cover and microwave on HIGH for 7 minutes until the sausages are cooked and the beans tender. Stir and reposition once during the cooking time.

Serves 4.

CHAPTER FIVE

Poultry and Game

Poultry can be cooked successfully in the microwave oven whether it is cut into pieces or whole. The only exception is a large whole turkey. Although the average microwave oven cavity is large enough to contain a well-shaped 18 lb (8 kg) turkey, the cooking process would be extremely uneven and turning the bird would present problems. The largest recommended size is 12 lb (5.6 kg).

Boiling chickens should be avoided unless they are to be used for stock, soup or in chopped dishes as they are likely to be tough. Roasting chickens and broiler-fryers produce excellent, flavorsome results.

Duck is always tougher and more chewy than chicken and so should be cooked for the majority of the time on a LOW setting. Although poultry does not brown appreciably in the microwave, duck flesh darkens as it cools, so that if you are preparing it for the freezer, the color will be just right when the dish is reheated. And if freshly cooked duck is served with a sauce it will look even more appetizing.

Duck is fatty and the fat should be spooned away during cooking. For this reason, it is best to cook a duck on a rack in a shallow dish, either cut up and cooked as quarters or roasted whole. Goose can be even fattier than duck and is usually roasted whole.

Prepare pheasant and other game birds in the usual way for cooking by microwave. Rabbit can be substituted for chicken in casseroles or where cooked meat is required in recipes.

Roast chicken

Fresh, young, free-range chickens produce the best flavor and the most tender flesh. They are available in specialty stores and some natural foods shops. Roasting chickens are best for cooking by microwave as it is almost impossible to tenderize a boiling fowl in the short cooking time. If the bird appears to have pockets of yellow fat, it may be unsuitable for microwaving as you will have to be continually spooning away the surplus melted fat as it accumulates. These fatty birds also shrink considerably while cooking.

There are various methods of microwave-roasting poultry. Chicken may be roasted either directly in a dish covered with a piece of waxed paper, or on an upturned, undecorated saucer in a dish, or on a special microwave roasting rack. The dish method is the easiest; the upturned saucer method is useful for an even-shaped bird although you may find that the saucer tends to stick to the dish. The roasting rack is a good idea if you have storage space for the rack when not in use and you do not object to the extra washing up.

Roasting bags are good for cooking lean birds but are unsuitable for fatty poultry. Cooking in a roasting bag enhances browning, although microwaved chicken will never be as brown as conventionally roasted chicken,

and the skin will remain moist. Roasting bags must never be sealed with the metal tag; the best way of closing the bag is to use a large elastic band leaving a wide gap.

Chicken may be cooked on HIGH, MEDIUM or LOW setting depending upon the dish you are cooking and the oven-to-table time you are able to allow. When chicken is cooked on HIGH, you will find that the leg and wing tips tend to overcook. These can be covered with small smooth pieces of foil halfway through cooking provided that the foil does not touch the sides or top of the oven. When the chicken is cooked on MEDIUM or in a roasting bag, shielding is not always necessary. Poultry can be roasted with stuffing loosely packed in the neck end only. If the stuffing is mainly sausage meat, it is advisable to microwave on MEDIUM or LOW to ensure that the stuffing cooks thoroughly. If you like the poultry to be browned, wipe with kitchen paper, then rub with butter and a coloring agent.

Except when using a roasting bag, a chicken should be cooked breast-side down for the first half of the cooking time. Large birds will cook more evenly if they are cooked for a quarter of the time on each of the four sides. Give the dish a turn occasionally.

Testing for doneness

If your oven is not fitted with a probe, use a microwave meat thermometer, or an ordinary meat thermometer when the chicken is removed from the microwave oven. If the chicken is not "tented" the temperature will not rise appreciably during standing time, so that you must cook to 185° F/85° C. The stuffing will register about 165° F/75° C depending on the content. Be sure to position the thermometer correctly (not alongside a bone).

To test for cooking without using a thermometer, insert the tip of a sharp knife close to the bone between the thigh and the body— if cooked no pink will remain and the juices will run clear. When the bone is twisted the leg should come away easily.

Chicken pieces

Chicken pieces are a useful standby particularly when one person requires just a quick supper. The sizes of chicken pieces vary considerably and those which are partially boned or boneless will cook much more quickly. On average a boneless chicken breast or drumstick will take 2–3 minutes while a quarter of a $3\frac{1}{4}$-lb (1.5-kg) chicken will take about 6 minutes.

If you remove the skin from chicken pieces, flavors and seasoning will penetrate the flesh better. Chicken with the skin on will take fractionally longer to cook. The shape of the chicken piece can make a difference to the timing so it is essential to test frequently whether it is cooked. The temperature of chicken pieces when tested with a thermometer does not always give a true reading, so test by twisting to see if the bone will move easily. The temperature does not rise appreciably after the chicken is removed from the microwave oven.

Because of the short cooking time, chicken pieces do not brown well but good results can be obtained using the browning dish or by coating in some way.

Chicken pieces should be thoroughly thawed before use; see chart on page 63. Cooking times must be adjusted according to weight, shape and number of pieces. Smaller, quicker-cooking quarters should be removed as soon as they are ready. Cook chicken pieces on HIGH.

Poultry pieces in sauce

Poultry can be cut into quarters or smaller pieces and be roasted either partly or fully before being finished with a sauce. The advantage of this is that there is no need to carve at the table and, if only one person wishes to eat, the other portions may be refrigerated or frozen for reheating later. Most of the sauces can be reheated with the poultry. A second advantage in cooking poultry when cut up is that it is possible to obtain very even results because the pieces can be repositioned and turned over much more easily than a whole bird.

Should you want to cook any of the following recipes using a single joint, remember to cut the cooking times down by at least two-thirds. Poultry portions can be tested with a meat thermometer but this is not entirely reliable since the thinner parts will cook before the thicker parts. Be sure to insert the point of the thermometer into the thickest part.

A $3\frac{1}{2}$-lb (1.6-kg) chicken cut into 8–12 pieces will take 18–24 minutes to cook. The pieces should be repositioned or stirred every 5 minutes and it is advantageous to give the dish a quarter-turn occasionally. Microwave covered with waxed paper to avoid splattering.

Casseroles

Do not hesitate to cook chicken casseroles in the microwave oven. They will be as tender and juicy as when cooked conventionally. Although not always strictly necessary, many conventional recipes recommend that chicken pieces be browned before cooking in a casserole and if you prefer to brown the chicken first, then do so

COOKING CHICKEN	
Casseroles	30–40 minutes on HIGH for 3-lb (1.5-kg) bird cut up, three-quarters covered.
Pieces	$2\frac{1}{2}$–$3\frac{1}{2}$ minutes on HIGH per piece; 6–9 minutes for 4 pieces.
Whole	9 minutes per 1 lb (450 g) on MEDIUM or 6 minutes on HIGH. Cover loosely. It is better to cook for half the time on HIGH, then the remaining time on MEDIUM.
DUCK	
Portions	4 × 11-oz (300-g) joints on HIGH for 10 minutes or on LOW for 30 minutes.
Whole	10 minutes per 1 lb (450 g) on MEDIUM or 7 minutes on HIGH. Cover with waxed paper.
GOOSE	1–$1\frac{1}{4}$ hours on HIGH for an average bird. Cook covered.
RABBIT	Cook as for chicken casseroles.
TURKEY	11–13 minutes per 1 lb (450 g) on MEDIUM or 9–11 minutes on HIGH. Cook in roasting bag.
VENISON	15 minutes for 4 cutlets on HIGH.

Thawing Poultry

either conventionally in a frying pan or if the chicken pieces are small they can be browned successfully in the browning dish. However many recipes will be equally succulent without pre-browning the chicken.

The cooking will be more even if the pieces are of equal size and thickness. Leg and side quarters are thicker than breast and wing quarters and will cook more evenly if they are cut into two pieces. Although the skin, wing tips and leg tips add to the quality of the gravy, producing a more jellied stock, you may prefer to remove these for the sake of appearance. The skin also produces extra fat and if you decide to leave it on you may have to skim the fat from the top of the casserole before serving.

Casseroles should be cooked covered and be stirred during cooking so that the uppermost and outer pieces do not become dry and overcooked. A chicken casserole may be microwaved on HIGH when cooked in a large amount of liquid. If there is little sauce then it is better to microwave on LOW; this will take more than twice as long but you can expect the flesh to be softer. When in a hurry for an almost instant meal, microwave on HIGH in half the given quantity of liquid or stock, adding the remainder after three-quarters of the cooking time. When casseroles are cooked in a small amount of liquid be careful to stir and scrape around the edges to prevent the sauce becoming lumpy and sticking against the sides of the dish. Leave to stand covered for 10 minutes and stir thoroughly before serving.

On average a chicken casserole takes 30–45 minutes to cook. The flavor of all casseroles improves if the dish is cooled rapidly, refrigerated for 24 hours and then reheated before serving. Do not leave the casserole to cool at room temperature but immerse the base in ice cold water and stir to assist the cooling process. When reheating be sure that the mixture comes to boiling point. For variety,

buy turkey pieces and casserole these in the same way.

Cooked chicken or turkey

Any recipe using cooked chicken or turkey must be reheated thoroughly. Add the chicken to the remaining ingredients halfway through cooking if there is a lot of sauce but three-quarters of the way through cooking if the sauce is minimal. Although most cooked chicken or turkey dishes are designed for using up leftovers, now that you have the microwave oven you can enjoy these dishes at any time by simply and quickly cooking the quantity that you require in the microwave oven prior to use. Be sure not to overcook the poultry as further cooking will take place during the time it takes to reheat it with the other ingredients. Cook the pieces thoroughly if they are going to be used in a cold dish such as Turkey and Ham terrine (see page 74).

Frozen poultry must be completely thawed before cooking. If doing this in the microwave oven, defrost until just a few ice crystals remain inside. Finish thawing in a large bowl of cold clear water until no ice crystals are left.

Chicken livers

Frozen chicken livers are often sold in tubs or blocks. Because they deteriorate quickly after thawing, buy only the quantity you require.

Thaw chicken livers before cooking. To do this, remove the frozen block from the container and put into a dish. Cover with a thick wad of paper towels which will soak up some of the excess liquid during thawing. Do not place the frozen block on top of paper towels as the liver will stick to the paper. Thaw in the refrigerator or according to the chart opposite.

Because chicken livers are enclosed in a skin, they will pop during cooking. Cut them in half to help avoid this and remove any pieces of white sinew. Always cook chicken livers covered. If they are cooked in liquid it does not matter whether you use a lid or perforated plastic wrap, but when sautéeing they should be covered with waxed paper. This prevents too much moisture being trapped, causing the livers to sweat rather than sauté.

The livers are ready when they are still just pink inside but no pink liquid runs. Stir frequently during cooking but do not overcook. Because they are so small cooking continues rapidly after the microwave oven is switched off.

Thawing Poultry and Game

THAWING CHICKEN

Casseroles	15 minutes, on HIGH, three-quarters covered.
Drumsticks	4 minutes per 1 lb (450 g) on LOW placed on rack, then in cold water for 15 minutes.
Legs and thighs	4 minutes per 1 lb (450 g) on LOW, then in cold water for 15 minutes.
Wings	7 minutes per 1 lb (450 g) on LOW, then in cold water 15 minutes.
Whole	6 minutes per 1 lb (450 g) on LOW. Remove giblets and neck as soon as they are free (if they are inside the bird) and use them for making stock or gravy.
Chicken livers	20 seconds on LOW, turn over then microwave for further 20 seconds. Leave to fully thaw at room temperature.

DUCK

Portions	4 minutes per 1 lb (450 g) on LOW, then in cold water for 15 minutes.
Whole	6 minutes per 1 lb (450 g) on LOW. 30–40 minutes for an average sized bird.

GOOSE	5 minutes per 1 lb (450 g) on LOW. Average bird takes 45 minutes.
RABBIT	10 minutes per 1 lb (450 g) on LOW, covered.
TURKEY	10–12 minutes per 1 lb (450 g) on LOW.
VENISON	10 minutes per 1 lb (450 g) on LOW.

Note On ovens with a 10% or WARM setting, almost double the thawing times, but the thawing will be more even (thawing should still be completed by immersing in cold water).

Thawing Whole Chicken or Duck

1

Cut away any metal clip and open the end of the wrapping. Make a slit in the bag along the back bone, under the bird, to let out the juices.

2

Put the bird breast-side up on an upturned, undecorated saucer or dish in a large shallow dish. Microwave on LOW or DEFROST for half the thawing time given on the chart (page 63).

3

Remove the wrappings and giblets as soon as they loosen. Drain any liquid from the dish. Turn the bird breast-side down and continue microwaving.

4

Feel the bird and shield with small, smooth pieces of foil any parts that are warm to touch, including wing tips and legs if their color seems to be changing. Be careful that the foil does not touch lining of oven.

5

Continue microwaving until just a few ice crystals remain inside. Remove the foil and immerse the bird in a bowl of cold water until no ice crystals remain inside. To double test, insert a small, sharp knife into the thickest part of the thigh. If it goes in easily the bird is fully thawed.

Thawing Whole Turkey

1

Remove any metal clips or tags, slit the bag underneath the bird and place the bird on a rack in a shallow dish. Microwave on the lowest possible setting.

2

Turn the bird over and give the dish a quarter-turn several times during thawing so that it has an equal amount of time on breast, back and sides. Follow each defrosting period with a 10–20 minute rest.

3

Remove the bag of giblets and outer wrappings as soon as they loosen.

4

Microwave according to the chart until half thawed. If shielding warm parts with foil is necessary, overwrap with plastic wrap to prevent the foil touching the oven lining.

5

When half thawed, leave the turkey at room temperature well away from any other meats (particularly cooked meats) and leave to finish thawing.

Giblets when being used for stock or soup may be cooked from frozen.

Thawing Poultry pieces

1

Remove from the packaging—do not thaw on a Styrofoam container. Separate the pieces as soon as possible if they are stuck together.

2

Place on a plate or in a shallow dish, thick sides toward the outside.

3

Microwave on LOW or DEFROST according to the chart timing, turning the pieces over and repositioning two or three times during thawing.

4

Small single poultry joints must *not* be shielded with foil. Finish thawing in cold water. When thawing several pieces at the same time, shield any parts which feel warm with small pieces of smooth foil. Remove any thawed pieces as soon as they are ready.

Chicken and Mushroom Casserole (page 68) in a round Pyrex casserole, and *overleaf,* **Chicken Liver and Port Pâté (page 73)**

Roast Chicken in a Baking Dish

1

Thaw frozen poultry completely. Wash thawed, frozen or fresh bird inside and out, shake out excess water and dry with paper towels.

2

Season inside the cavity with salt and pepper and place half an onion inside, or stuff the neck end loosely.

3

Tuck the wings underneath and legs close to the sides of the chicken. Tie the legs together with string.

4

Rub with butter and paprika or Worcestershire sauce, gravy browning, tomato ketchup or gravy powder (or a special microwave browning agent).

5

Put the prepared chicken breast side down in large shallow dish. Cover with waxed paper.

6

Microwave on HIGH for half the cooking time. Give dish a half-turn halfway through the cooking period.

7

Turn the chicken breast side up, replace the waxed paper and microwave on MEDIUM or LOW for the remaining cooking time.

8

If preferred, insert a microwave thermometer into the thicker part of the thigh. An ordinary meat thermometer is not suitable.

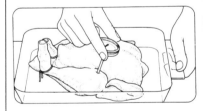

9

Shield any less meaty parts such as leg and wing tips as soon as they are cooked, making sure the foil does not touch the oven lining.

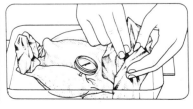

10

As soon as the chicken is ready remove from the microwave oven and tent with foil. Leave to stand for 15 minutes.

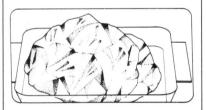

Note This method is perfectly adequate for an everyday roast or when the meat is required subsequently in a made-up chicken dish.

Roast chicken using an upturned undecorated saucer: Cook as above but put the chicken on an inverted undecorated saucer in a shallow dish. This helps keep the chicken out of its cooking juices, encouraging it to roast rather than braise.

Roast chicken using a roasting rack: Cook as above but remove the chicken and rack halfway through cooking and pour away excess fat. Then replace the chicken and rack and continue cooking.

Cooking Poultry in a Roasting Bag

1

Place the chicken, breast side up, in the roasting bag.

2

Tie the end loosely with string or a large elastic band, leaving a gap at the top.

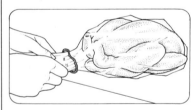

3

Microwave on HIGH for half the time and MEDIUM or LOW for the remaining time. Give the dish a quarter-turn four times during cooking.

Microwaving chicken with a temperature probe
Insert the probe through the roasting bag into the thickest part of the thigh. Follow the manufacturer's instructions for the recommended temperature setting.

Gravy for Turkey or Chicken

giblets from 1 turkey or
  chicken
1 level Tbsp (15 ml) cornstarch

1

Put the giblets in a 3-quart (2.8-l) bowl with 2¼ cups (450 ml) water. If including the chicken livers, prick or halve first so that they do not explode. Three-quarters cover with plastic wrap and microwave on HIGH for 30 minutes. Allow an extra 15 minutes if the giblets were still frozen. Strain.

2

Blend the cornstarch with 3–4 tsp (15–20 ml) cold water. Mix into the freshly cooked stock and make up to 2¼ cups (450 ml) with juices from the cooked poultry.

3

Microwave on HIGH for 3 minutes or until the gravy thickens. Stir occasionally during cooking. To give added color, add a few drops of gravy browning or a chicken bouillon cube.

Candida Chicken

3½-lb (1.6-kg) oven-ready chicken
3 Tbsp (40 g) butter, softened
½ green pepper, seeded and
  finely sliced
1 small onion, peeled and finely
  sliced
4 oz (125 g) small zucchini,
  trimmed and thinly sliced
2 tomatoes, chopped
1 level Tbsp (15 ml) tomato
  paste
¼ cup (25 g) fresh breadcrumbs
pinch of dried marjoram
little beaten egg
salt and freshly ground pepper

1

Rub the chicken with 1 Tbsp (15 g) of the butter. In a bowl mix the remaining butter with the green pepper, onion and zucchini. Cover and microwave on HIGH for 4 minutes or until the vegetables begin to soften. Stir occasionally during cooking.

2

Mix in the tomatoes, tomato paste, breadcrumbs, marjoram and enough egg to bind. Season to taste with salt and pepper.

3

Fill the neck with the stuffing and tuck the wings underneath. Place the chicken in an unsealed roasting bag in a large shallow dish. Microwave on HIGH for 12 minutes, giving the dish a quarter-turn four times during cooking.

4

Reduce the setting and microwave on LOW for 30 minutes or until the chicken is cooked.

5

Leave for 10 minutes, then slit the roasting bag and transfer the chicken to a carving dish. Carve the chicken and arrange it with the stuffing on a warmed serving dish.

Serves 4–6.

Chicken Divan

3-lb (1.4-kg) oven-ready chicken
2–3 large rosemary sprigs
salt and freshly ground pepper
2 Tbsp (25 g) butter or margarine
2 level Tbsp (30 ml) all-purpose
    flour
1 cup (240 ml) milk
grated rind and juice of $\frac{1}{2}$ lemon
1 egg yolk
5 Tbsp (75 ml) mayonnaise
3 level Tbsp (45 ml) grated
    Parmesan cheese
8–12 oz (225–350 g)
    frozen broccoli spears or
    florets of fresh broccoli

1

Put the chicken, rosemary sprigs, salt, pepper and $\frac{1}{2}$ cup (120 ml) water into a large roasting bag and place in a large shallow dish.

2

Loosely close the roasting bag with a large elastic band, leaving a big opening. The bag need not be upright but must not touch the walls or top of the oven, which could tip it over.

3

Turn the bag over so that the chicken is breast side down and microwave on HIGH for 10 minutes, giving the dish a quarter-turn four times during cooking.

4

Using oven gloves carefully turn the bag over so that the chicken is breast-side up. Reduce the power and microwave on LOW for 25 minutes or until the chicken is cooked. Give the dish a quarter-turn four times during cooking.

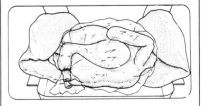

5

Leave to stand for 10 minutes, then take the chicken carefully out of the bag. Strain the cooking liquid into a cup and skim the fat away from the surface.

6

Put the butter in a medium bowl and microwave on HIGH for 45 seconds. Stir in the flour and blend in the milk and $\frac{2}{3}$ cup (150 ml) of the reserved cooking liquid. Beat in the lemon rind, juice, egg yolk, mayonnaise and the cheese. Microwave on HIGH, whisking vigorously every 30 seconds, for 3 minutes or until the sauce thickens.

7

Put the broccoli into the roasting bag with 3 Tbsp (45 ml) water and microwave on HIGH for 4 minutes. Drain. Remove the bones and skin from the chicken and arrange the chicken pieces in the cooking dish.

8

Cover with the broccoli and pour the sauce over the top. Cover with the lid or plastic wrap and microwave on HIGH for 4 minutes or until thoroughly hot. Give the dish an occasional turn and stir around the edges of the sauce during reheating.

Serves 4–6.

Crumbed Chicken

1 chicken quarter, skinned
salt and freshly ground pepper
all-purpose flour
beaten egg
$\frac{1}{3}$ cup (40 g) light breadcrumbs
1 Tbsp (15 ml) vegetable oil

1

Season the chicken with salt and pepper and coat with flour, shaking off the surplus.

2

Dip the floured chicken joint in the beaten egg, then coat with the breadcrumbs.

3

Put the oil in a shallow dish and microwave on HIGH for 30 seconds.

4

Put the chicken in the dish fleshy side down, cover with waxed paper and microwave on HIGH for 3 minutes.

5

Turn the chicken over, cover with the waxed paper and microwave on HIGH for 3 minutes or until cooked. The chicken should be tender when tested, with no pink near the bone.

Serves 1.

Marinated Chicken in Teriyaki Sauce

4 Tbsp (60 ml) soy sauce
4 Tbsp (60 ml) light honey
6 Tbsp (90 ml) dry sherry
$\frac{1}{4}$ level tsp (1.25 ml) ground
   ginger
1 small clove garlic, peeled and
   crushed
$\frac{1}{4}$ level tsp (1.25 ml) salt
$3\frac{1}{2}$-lb (1.6-kg) oven-ready
   chicken
2 level Tbsp (30 ml) cornstarch

1

Put the soy sauce, honey, sherry, ginger, garlic and salt in a large roasting bag and microwave on HIGH, unsealed and upright, for 1 minute or until the honey melts.

2

Using oven gloves, shake the bag gently to combine the ingredients.

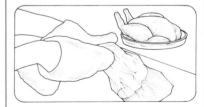

3

Put the chicken in the bag and seal securely. Stand the bag in a shallow dish, turn the bag over once to coat the chicken with the marinade, then leave for 2 hours, turning the bag and the chicken occasionally to cover well.

4

Turn the roasting bag so that the chicken is breast side up and remove the seal. Replace with a large elastic band, leaving a big gap so that steam can escape. Microwave on HIGH for 20 minutes or until the chicken is cooked. Give the dish a half-turn halfway through cooking.

5

Leave to stand for 10 minutes, then test again to make sure that the chicken is completely cooked. A thermometer or sharp knife can be plunged through the roasting bag to do this.

6

Slit the bag down the center and place the chicken in a warm serving dish.

7

Carefully remove the roasting bag, allowing the juices to run into the cooking dish. Remove surplus fat.

8

Mix the cornstarch with 1 Tbsp (15 ml) cold water. Stir into the juices in the dish. Microwave on HIGH for 2 minutes or until the sauce thickens, stirring vigorously once or twice. Pour the sauce over the chicken and serve hot.

Serve 4–6.

Chicken and Mushroom Casserole

2 medium onions, peeled and
   finely chopped
1 clove garlic, peeled and
   crushed
1 Tbsp (15 ml) vegetable oil
2 Tbsp (25 g) all-purpose flour
$3\frac{1}{2}$-lb (1.6-kg) oven-ready
   chicken, skinned and cut into
   8 or 12 pieces
$1\frac{1}{4}$ cups (300 ml) red wine
8-oz (225-g) can tomatoes
6 oz (175 g) mushrooms, sliced
1 Tbsp (15 ml) chopped fresh
   parsley
2 bay leaves
salt and freshly ground pepper

1

Put the onions, garlic and oil into a deep casserole and microwave on HIGH for 8 minutes or until the onions start to brown. Stir once or twice during cooking.

2

Stir in the flour then add the chicken and all the remaining ingredients.

3

Cover with a lid and microwave on HIGH for 25 minutes, repositioning the chicken twice during cooking.

4

Reduce power and microwave on LOW for 15 minutes or until the chicken is cooked. Reposition once during this cooking period. Leave to stand, covered, for 10 minutes before serving.

Serves 4–6.

Note It may be necessary to add more liquid halfway through the cooking period and it is a good idea to stir round the edges of the sauce when repositioning the chicken. At the end of the cooking time, if the sauce is too thin, thicken with 1 level tsp (5 ml) cornstarch blended with 2 Tbsp (30 ml) cold water, return the casserole to the microwave oven uncovered and microwave on HIGH until boiling.

Chicken in Barbecue Sauce

4½-lb (2-kg) oven-ready chicken

For the stuffing
dab of butter
1 small onion, peeled and finely chopped
½ celery stalk, trimmed and finely chopped
2 oz (50 g) sausage meat
1 cooking apple, peeled and chopped
¼ cup (25 g) fresh breadcrumbs
1 tsp (5 ml) chopped fresh parsley
salt and freshly ground pepper
little beaten egg

1

To make the stuffing, put the butter, onion and celery in a large bowl, cover and microwave on HIGH for 3 minutes or until the onions are soft but not colored. Stir once during cooking.

2

Add the sausage meat and cooking apple to the onion mixture, stir well, cover and microwave on HIGH for 2 minutes or until the apple is soft, and the sausage meat partly cooked.

3

Mix in the breadcrumbs, parsley, salt, pepper and bind with the beaten egg.

4

Fill the neck of the chicken with the stuffing and tuck the wings underneath. Put the chicken breast side down in a shallow dish.

5

To make the sauce, combine all the ingredients in a large cup. Mix thoroughly, making sure that the cornstarch does not stick on the bottom of the cup. Microwave on HIGH for 30 seconds, then stir and microwave on HIGH for 1 minute or until the sauce thickens slightly. Beat thoroughly.

For the sauce
5 Tbsp (75 ml) red wine
4 Tbsp (60 ml) chicken stock or water
1 tsp (5 ml) soy sauce
2 Tbsp (30 ml) red wine vinegar
1 tsp (5 ml) Worcestershire sauce
1 level Tbsp (15 ml) tomato paste
1 level tsp (5 ml) Dijon-style mustard
1 level Tbsp (15 ml) light brown sugar
1 level tsp (5 ml) cornstarch

6

Pour the sauce over the chicken, cover with a lid or waxed paper and microwave on HIGH for 15 minutes, giving the dish a quarter-turn every 3–4 minutes.

7

Turn the chicken over carefully and microwave on HIGH for 15 minutes, basting once during cooking. Give the dish a half-turn and reduce the setting, then microwave on LOW for 25 minutes or until the chicken is cooked.

8

Test, then tent with foil and leave for 10–15 minutes before serving.

9

Lift the chicken on to a serving dish and spoon away any surplus fat from the sauce. Reheat the sauce either in the cooking dish or in a cup, microwaving on HIGH for 1–2 minutes.

Serves 6–8.

Curried Chicken

2 large onions, peeled and finely chopped
4 Tbsp (60 ml) vegetable oil
2 level tsp (10 ml) cumin
¼ level tsp (1.25 ml) cinnamon
2 level tsp (10 ml) cardamom
¼ level tsp (1.25 ml) ground bayleaves
freshly ground black pepper
¼ level tsp (1.25 ml) ginger
1 clove garlic, crushed
14-oz (397-g) can tomatoes
3½-lb (1.6-kg) oven-ready chicken, skinned and cut into 8 pieces
1 level tsp (5 ml) salt

1

To make the curry sauce, combine the onion, oil, spices and garlic in a large, deep casserole. Microwave on HIGH for 10 minutes or until the onion is just browning. Stir frequently during cooking.

2

Add the tomatoes and their juice, the chicken pieces and the salt.

3

Cover with the lid and microwave on HIGH for 25 minutes or until the chicken is tender. Stir and reposition the chicken at least twice during cooking.

4

Leave to stand, covered, for 10 minutes before serving.

Serves 4–6.

Note The flavor of curry improves if the dish is cooled quickly, refrigerated for 24 hours and reheated thoroughly before serving.

Italian Chicken

1 Tbsp (15 ml) olive oil
1 Tbsp (15 g) butter or
    margarine
4 chicken joints, wiped
$\frac{1}{2}$ green pepper, seeded and
    sliced
$\frac{1}{2}$ red pepper, seeded and
    sliced
8-oz (227-g) can tomatoes
1 clove garlic, peeled and
    crushed
1 level tsp (5 ml) dried basil
6 Tbsp (90 ml) red wine
salt and freshly ground pepper
1 level Tbsp (15 ml) cornstarch

1

Preheat the browning dish to
maximum, according to the
manufacturer's instructions,
adding the oil and butter for the
last 15 seconds.

2

Without removing the dish from
the oven, quickly place the chicken
pieces, skin side down, in the hot
butter mixture. Microwave on
HIGH for 3 minutes, then turn the
pieces over.

3

Stir in the peppers, tomatoes with
their juice, garlic, basil and red
wine. Cover with the lid and
continue to cook on HIGH for 12
minutes, repositioning the chicken
twice.

4

Reduce the setting to LOW and
cook for a further 10 minutes or
until the chicken is tender.

5

Remove the pieces to a warmed
serving dish. Blend the cornstarch
to a paste with a little cold water
and stir into the juices. Microwave
on HIGH for 5 minutes, stirring
once. Pour over the chicken.

Serves 4.

Chicken and Mushroom Scallops

4 oz (100 g) mushrooms, finely
    sliced
2 level Tbsp (30 ml) canned
    corn
2 Tbsp (25 g) butter or
    margarine
2 Tbsp (25 g) all-purpose flour
$\frac{2}{3}$ cup (150 ml) chicken stock
3 Tbsp (45 ml) heavy cream,
    whipped
8 oz (225 g) cooked chicken,
    finely chopped
salt and freshly ground pepper
1 lb (450 g) potato, cooked and
    mashed

1

Put the mushrooms and corn on a
plate or in a dish, cover and
microwave on HIGH for 3 minutes
or until the mushrooms are soft.

2

Put the butter in a medium bowl
and microwave on HIGH for 45
seconds or until melted. Stir in the
flour and gradually beat in the
stock.

3

Microwave on HIGH for 2–3
minutes, whisking after the first
minute then frequently until the
sauce is very thick.

4

Stir in the cream, then mix in the
chicken, mushrooms and corn,
adding their cooking liquid. Season
to taste with salt and pepper.

5

Divide the mixture between 4
scallop shells and pipe a decorative
border of mashed potato around
the edges. Reheat in the
microwave oven on HIGH for
about 5 minutes and brown under
the broiler if you wish.

Serves 4 as a starter.

Chicken à la King

$\frac{1}{4}$ cup (50 g) butter or margarine
$\frac{1}{4}$ green pepper, seeded and
    finely chopped
$\frac{1}{4}$ red pepper, seeded and finely
    chopped
$\frac{1}{4}$ cup (40 g) all-purpose flour
$2\frac{1}{4}$ cups (450 ml) milk
$\frac{1}{2}$ chicken bouillon cube,
    crumbled
2 tsp (10 ml) sherry
4 oz (100 g) button mushrooms,
    wiped and thinly sliced
salt and freshly ground pepper
8–12 oz (225–350 g) cooked
    chicken, cut in small pieces
2 Tbsp (30 ml) heavy cream

1

Put the butter in a casserole and
microwave on HIGH for 1 minute
or until melted.

2

Stir in the green and red pepper.
Cover and microwave on HIGH for
2 minutes, stirring once during
cooking.

3

Stir in the flour, milk, crumbled
bouillon cube and sherry. Add the
mushrooms, three-quarters cover
with plastic wrap and microwave
on HIGH for 4 minutes or until the
mushrooms are soft. Stir
occasionally during cooking.

4

Season to taste with pepper,
adding salt only if necessary. Stir in
the chicken and the cream. Three-
quarters cover and microwave on
HIGH for 5 minutes or until the
chicken is hot. Stir two or three
times through the gap in the
plastic wrap during cooking,
making sure to draw any
coagulating sauce away from the
sides and into the mixture. Serve
with boiled rice or green
tagliatelle.

Serves 4.

Walnut and Yogurt Chicken

3-lb (1.4-kg) oven-ready
  chicken, cut into 8 pieces
2 Tbsp (25 g) wholewheat flour
1 Tbsp (15 g) butter or
  margarine
$\frac{1}{2}$ level tsp (2.5 ml) salt
$\frac{1}{4}$ level tsp (1.25 ml) pepper
$\frac{2}{3}$ cup (150 ml) yogurt
$\frac{1}{4}$ cup (25 g) finely chopped
  walnuts
2 level tsp (10 ml) paprika
pinch of garlic salt
1 level Tbsp (15 ml) sesame
  seeds
watercress to garnish

1

Dip the chicken pieces in the flour
and shake off the surplus.

2

Put the butter, salt and pepper in a
large shallow dish and microwave
on HIGH for 45 seconds or until
the butter is melted. Stir to mix
the seasoning evenly.

3

Put the chicken pieces into the
melted butter and turn them over
so that they are lightly coated.

4

Cover with waxed paper and
microwave on HIGH for 20
minutes or until cooked.
Reposition the chicken twice
during cooking.

5

Combine the yogurt, walnuts,
paprika, garlic salt and sesame
seeds. Spoon over the chicken and
microwave on LOW without
covering, for 5 minutes or until
hot. Give the dish a quarter-turn
every minute during reheating.

6

Garnish with watercress and serve
at once.

Serves 4.

Stuffed Chicken Thighs or Drumsticks

$\frac{1}{4}$ cup (25 g) dry stuffing mix
8 chicken thighs or drumsticks,
  skinned and boned
2 Tbsp (25 g) butter or
  margarine, softened
1 level tsp (5 ml) paprika
$\frac{1}{2}$ level tsp (2.5 ml) salt
$\frac{1}{4}$ level tsp (1.25 ml) pepper

1

Reconstitute the stuffing according
to the directions on the packet.

2

Divide the stuffing into equal
portions and press onto each
chicken piece. Press edges
together and secure with
toothpicks.

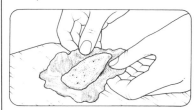

3

Mix together the butter, paprika,
salt and pepper. Rub the chicken
with the softened paprika butter
and place the pieces, seam side
down, in a shallow dish. Cover
lightly with waxed paper and
microwave on HIGH for 15
minutes or until cooked.
Reposition the chicken pieces two
or three times during cooking.

Serves 4.

Note Be sure to test for cooking
on both sides of the poultry. A
thermometer inserted into the
stuffing may not give a true
reading.

"Stir-fried" Turkey

8 oz (225 g) turkey fillet
1 Tbsp (15 ml) vegetable oil
2 Tbsp (30 ml) soy sauce
2 Tbsp (30 ml) dry sherry
$\frac{1}{2}$ level tsp (2.5 ml) ground
  ginger
$\frac{1}{2}$ green pepper, seeded and
  sliced
4 spring onions, peeled and
  chopped
4 oz (125 g) beansprouts

1

Cut the turkey fillet into strips and
put in a bowl. Add the oil, soy
sauce and sherry and stir. Leave to
marinate for about 30 minutes.

2

Preheat a browning dish to
maximum according to the
manufacturer's instructions. Stir in
the turkey strips, then add the
marinade and ginger and stir
quickly to seal the meat. Add the
pepper and onions and microwave
on HIGH for 2 minutes.

3

Stir in the beansprouts and
microwave on HIGH for a further 2
minutes. Serve at once with rice
and soy sauce.

Serves 2.

Note This dish can also be made
without a browning dish. Allow
about 1–2 minutes extra cooking
time and test the turkey for
tenderness.

Duck à l'Orange

2 ducklings, quartered
vegetable oil

For the sauce
3 large oranges
about $\frac{1}{3}$ cup (75 ml) red wine
1 level Tbsp (15 ml) cornstarch
2 Tbsp (30 ml) orange
    marmalade
salt and freshly ground pepper

1

Place the ducks skin side up on a roasting rack in a large shallow dish.

2

Brush the skin lightly all over with the vegetable oil. Cover with waxed paper and microwave on HIGH for 10 minutes, giving the dish a quarter-turn three times during cooking.

3

Re-arrange the duck pieces so that the outer sides are in the middle, then reduce the setting and microwave on LOW for 30 minutes, repositioning the duck pieces and giving the dish a quarter turn three times during cooking.

4

Meanwhile, start to prepare the sauce. Grate the rind from the oranges, squeeze the juice from 2 of them and pour into a measuring cup. Remove the peel and pith from the other orange, cut into segments and reserve for garnish.

5

Remove the duck pieces to a flameproof serving dish, crisp under a hot grill, and keep warm.

6

Remove the roasting rack. Tilt the dish and pour away all but 1 Tbsp (15 ml) duck fat. Put this into a $1\frac{1}{2}$-pint (0.85 litre) bowl. Stir the remaining duck juices into the cup with the orange juice and make up to $1\frac{1}{4}$ cups (300 ml) with red wine.

7

Stir the cornstarch into the fat in the bowl, add the orange juice and wine mixture and marmalade and microwave on HIGH for 5 minutes, stirring occasionally. Season with salt and pepper. Arrange the duck on a hot serving dish, pour the sauce over the top and garnish with the orange segments.

Serves 4.

Note Duck must be microwaved on a roasting rack because of the large amount of fat that comes from it. A $2\frac{3}{4}$-lb (1.2-kg) duck can produce more than $\frac{2}{3}$ cup (150 ml) fat.

  To separate the juices from the fat most efficiently pour both into a freezer or roasting bag. Hold the bag so one corner is filled, then, having a cup and a large bowl at the ready, snip the tip off the filled corner. Allow the juices which will be in the bottom of the bag to run into the cup. Quickly grasp the open end before any fat escapes and put the whole bag with the fat into the bowl.

Pheasant in White Wine

1 brace oven-ready pheasants,
    cut in half along backbone
salt and freshly ground pepper
1 medium onion, peeled and
    finely sliced
1 orange, peeled and
    segmented, reserving the
    peel
$1\frac{1}{4}$ cups (300 ml) dry white wine
2 Tbsp (30 ml) brandy
2 level Tbsp (30 ml) cornstarch

1

Season pheasant halves with salt and pepper and place skin side down in a casserole. Arrange thicker parts toward outside of dish.

2

Cover with the onion slices and orange segments. Gradually stir the wine and brandy into the cornstarch so that it is evenly blended, then pour over the pheasants.

3

Cover with a lid and microwave on HIGH for 10 minutes. Turn and reposition the pheasant portions.

4

Meanwhile, pare the pith away from the reserved orange peel and cut the rind into matchstick strips. Put these strips into a large cup, cover with cold water and microwave on HIGH for 1 minute or until boiling. Drain, then repeat and drain again.

5

Add the orange strips to the casserole and microwave on HIGH for 10 minutes or until the pheasants are cooked. Give the dish a quarter-turn four times during cooking.

Serves 4.

Mustard Rabbit Casserole

1 rabbit, about 2½ lb (1 kg), cut up
2 level Tbsp (30 ml) all-purpose flour
salt and freshly ground pepper
2 medium onions, peeled and finely sliced
2 large carrots, peeled and sliced
2–3 level Tbsp (30–45 ml) Dijon-style mustard
1¼ cups (300 ml) chicken stock
⅔ cup (150 ml) dry cider
1 level tsp (5 ml) dried thyme

1

Wash the rabbit pieces well and pat dry with paper towels. Coat in the flour seasoned with salt and pepper.

2

Put the rabbit, onions and carrots in a 3-quart (3-litre) casserole. Stir the mustard into the stock and cider and pour over the rabbit. Sprinkle over the thyme. Cover the casserole.

3

Microwave on HIGH for 15 minutes, turning and repositioning the rabbit twice. Reduce the setting to MEDIUM and cook for a further 35 minutes or until the rabbit is tender. Reposition the rabbit joints twice during the cooking time. Serve with Red cabbage and apple casserole (see page 83).

Serves 4.

Note If time permits place the rabbit pieces, onions, carrots, thyme, mustard, stock and cider in the casserole and marinate overnight. Blend the flour to a paste with a little water and add before cooking.

Chicken Liver and Port Pâté

1 lb (450 g) chicken livers
5 Tbsp (75 ml) dry white wine
1½ cups (350 g) butter
½ level tsp (2.5 ml) salt
¼ level tsp (1.25 ml) freshly ground black pepper
½ level tsp (2.5 ml) ground mixed spice
4 Tbsp (60 ml) port wine
cherries to garnish

1

Rinse the chicken livers in cold water and cut in half to prevent popping.

2

Put the wine in a medium bowl and microwave on HIGH for 1½ minutes or until fully boiling.

3

Stir in the chicken livers and three-quarters cover with plastic wrap. Microwave on HIGH, stirring occasionally, for 6 minutes or until the livers are just cooked but still pink-brown inside.

4

Transfer the livers to a blender or food processor using a slotted spoon and add 2 Tbsp (30 ml) of the cooking liquor (save the remaining liquor for use in stocks and gravies).

5

Add 1¼ cups (275 g) of the butter, salt, pepper, mixed spice and the port and blend until smooth. Spoon into a 2½-cup (600-ml) pâté dish. Chill until firm.

6

Put the remaining butter in a small dish and cover with waxed paper. Microwave on HIGH for 45 seconds or until melted.

7

Garnish the pâté with cherries. Being careful to exclude any sediment, strain the melted butter evenly over the top of the pâté. Chill until the butter is set.

Serves 8–12.

Note The pâté can be spooned into 8 individual ramekins if preferred.

Turkey and Ham Terrine

8 oz (225 g) skinned cooked turkey
8 oz (225 g) cooked ham
1 onion, peeled and minced
2 tsp (10 ml) chopped fresh sage
salt and freshly ground pepper
1 chicken bouillon cube, crumbled
2 level Tbsp (30 ml) gelatin
1¼ cups (300 ml) heavy cream, whipped

For the topping
1½ level tsp (7.5 ml) gelatin
1 cup (240 ml) mayonnaise
6–8 green olives, pitted and sliced

1

Mince or finely chop the cooked turkey and cooked ham together. Thoroughly mix the onion and herbs into the meat mixture and season to taste with salt and pepper.

2

Heat 2½ cups (600 ml) water either in the kettle or in a bowl in the microwave oven on HIGH. When the water is very hot but not boiling, add the crumbled chicken bouillon cube, stir thoroughly then sprinkle the gelatin over the surface. Stir until dissolved. Leave to cool.

3

Pour the cooled stock into the turkey mixture and when it begins to thicken, fold in the whipped cream.

4

Spoon into an 11-inch (28-cm) loaf-shaped dish. Leave to set in the refrigerator.

5

Dip the base of the dish into hot water for a few seconds to release the terrine and turn it out on to a wire rack over a tray.

6

Put 5 Tbsp (75 ml) water in a 2½-cup (600-ml) bowl and microwave on HIGH for 45 seconds or until nearly boiling. Remove from the microwave oven and sprinkle on the 1½ level tsp (7.5 ml) gelatin. Stir until dissolved. Leave to cool but not thicken.

7

Stir the cooled gelatin into the mayonnaise. Pour evenly over the terrine, allowing the surplus to drain into the tray.

8

Garnish with a line of green olives. Transfer to a serving dish and refrigerate until the mayonnaise coating is set.

Serves 12.

Chicken with Mushrooms and Almonds

2 oz (50 g) flaked almonds
4 chicken breasts, weighing 8 oz (225 g) each, skinned and boned
2 Tbsp (25 g) butter
4 oz (100 g) mushrooms, wiped and sliced
⅔ cup (150 ml) light cream
salt and freshly ground pepper

1

Spread the almonds in one layer on a pie plate and microwave on HIGH for 5 minutes or until golden brown. Move the almonds around on the plate twice during the cooking time to prevent them burning in the center. Leave to cool.

2

Place the chicken breasts between sheets of waxed paper or foil and beat flat.

3

Put the butter in a shallow dish large enough to hold the chicken breasts in a single layer and microwave on HIGH for 45 seconds until melted.

4

Add the chicken breasts and turn over to coat in the butter. Cover with plastic wrap and microwave on HIGH for 12 minutes or until tender.

5

Push the chicken to one side of the dish, add the mushrooms and stir to coat in the juices. Recover and microwave on HIGH for 3 minutes until the mushrooms are cooked. Add the cream, seasoning and the almonds and stir well. Cover and microwave on HIGH for 2 minutes until sauce is hot but not bubbling.

Serves 4.

CHAPTER SIX

Vegetables

Microwaved vegetables have a good texture and color, are full of taste and retain more vitamins than when they are cooked conventionally. Vegetables also respond well to reheating in the microwave oven.

Pierce or score the skins of shiny vegetables such as eggplants, peppers or tomatoes and thoroughly prick potatoes when they are to be cooked in their jackets. Evenly sliced or diced vegetables will cook more uniformly than whole or mis-shapen pieces. For example, sliced carrots will cook more quickly and successfully than whole carrots. When vegetables are cooked whole, arrange the thinner parts toward the center of the dish or overlap the thick and thin pieces to make an even layer. Vegetables cooked in water should be stirred or repositioned several times during cooking.

Never sprinkle salt directly on to raw vegetables before cooking. Salt distorts the microwave patterns and causes the vegetables to dry up. If appropriate, stir salt into the water before adding the vegetables.

Most fresh vegetables can be cooked on HIGH. High water content vegetables such as zucchini, mushrooms, spinach and tomatoes require no added liquid. Small podded vegetables such as peas, beans and corn kernels, require a small amount of water. Root vegetables require a larger amount of water and cooking times depend upon the age of the vegetable. Cauliflower is one of the most difficult vegetables to cook by microwave, since the stalk is much tougher than the florets. For best results break the cauliflower into separate florets and discard the tough stalk. However if cauliflower is required for soups or purées, it is quite in order to microwave it whole.

Fresh vegetables can be cooked very successfully in roasting bags, which must be only loosely sealed with a non-metallic fastening. Take care not to scald yourself when removing the vegetables from the roasting bag.

Blanching vegetables for the freezer

Use the microwave oven for blanching prior to freezing. A maximum of 1 lb (450 g) of pre-pared vegetables can be blanched at one time in 4–5 Tbsp (45–60 ml) water without added salt. Microwave on HIGH for 2 minutes, then stir and microwave on HIGH for 1–2 more minutes or until the vegetable pieces are all equally hot. Drain and plunge vegetables into ice-cold water, then drain and pack. Cauliflower and brussel sprouts need extra attention when stirring to make sure that they are thoroughly heated through. Otherwise they will become musty during freezer storage.

Frozen vegetables

All frozen vegetables may be cooked on a HIGH setting. Single portions of small vegetables such as peas, beans or corn kernels can be cooked without added water, as can spinach and mushrooms, which contain sufficient water themselves. Larger amounts should be cooked in a few tablespoons of salted water. The exception is corn on the cob which requires only butter or margarine.

Canned vegetables

Canned vegetables require reheating only. Drain and reheat on HIGH. Cover, particularly when whole vegetables are mixed in a sauce (eg, beans). General cooking instructions are given in the chart (overleaf) but cooking times vary depending upon the freshness, type, size, shape, dish and starting temperature of the canned vegetables.

Drying herbs

If you have no freezer or freezer compartment and you have bought or grown more herbs that you can use, the remainder can easily be dried in a microwave oven. Herbs dried this way keep their color and flavor well.

Be sure to stir and mix frequently during drying—every 20 seconds during the first minute and every 5–10 seconds thereafter—to prevent burning.

For specific information on drying herbs, see page 78.

Cooking Fresh Vegetables

All times are given as a guide only, since variations in size and quality will affect cooking times. Try to choose even-sized vegetables. Unless otherwise stated cook covered in 5–6 Tbsp (75–90 ml) salted water. Leave to stand for 3 minutes before draining off the water.

Vegetables	Preparation	Quantity	Approximate time on HIGH	Further instructions
Artichokes, globe	Wash and drain. Cut off stalk at base. Slice off upper tip and trim tips of leaves.	1 2 3	5–6 minutes 7–8 minutes 11–12 minutes	Place upright in covered dish.
Asparagus	Remove white woody part to give even length spears.	12 oz (350 g)	5–7 minutes	Place stalks toward outside of dish. Cooking time may vary with thickness and age.
Beans, broad	Shell.	1 lb (450 g)	6–8 minutes	Stir or shake after 3 minutes and test after 5 minutes.
Beans, green	String and slice or leave whole.	1 lb (450 g)	12–16 minutes	Stir or shake during cooking period. Time will vary with age and size.
Beets, medium, whole	Wash and pierce skin with fork.	4 medium	14–16 minutes	Re-arrange during cooking. Skin and remove stalks after cooking.
Broccoli	Wash, remove outer leaves and tough portion of stalk. Slit stem ends to speed up cooking.	1 lb (450 g)	10–12 minutes	Re-arrange during cooking.
Brussel sprouts	Discard outside wilted leaves. Trim and cut a cross in stalk end.	8 oz (225 g) 1 lb (450 g)	4–6 minutes 7–10 minutes	Stir or shake during cooking.
Cabbage, quartered	Discard damaged and wilted leaves. Trim stalk.	1 lb (450 g)	10–12 minutes	Stir or shake during cooking.
shredded		1 lb (450 g)	9–11 minutes	
Carrots	Scrape, or peel and slice.	8 oz (225 g) 1 lb (450 g)	7–8 minutes 10–12 minutes	Stir or shake during cooking.
Cauliflower	Whole. Trim, break into florets.	 8 oz (225 g) 1 lb (450 g)	12–16 minutes 7–8 minutes 10–12 minutes	Stir or shake during cooking. Do not sprinkle salt directly on to the vegetable.
Celery	Separate sticks and wash. Slice or cut into strips.	1 lb (450 g)	7–10 minutes	Stir or shake during cooking.
Corn-on-the-cob	Remove husk, wash and trim. Wrap individually in greased waxed paper. Do not add water.	2	6–8 minutes	Turn over after 3 minutes.
Eggplant	Wash, slice, sprinkle with salt and leave for 30 minutes. Rinse and pat dry.	1 lb (450 g) (2 medium)	8–10 minutes	Stir or shake after 4 minutes.

Vegetables	Preparation	Quantity	Approximate time on HIGH	Further instructions
Leeks	Wash very thoroughly, trim and slice.	1 lb (450 g)	10–12 minutes	Stir or shake during cooking.
Mushrooms	Trim stalks. Wipe. Do not add water. Add 2 Tbsp (25 g) butter and a squeeze of lemon juice.	8 oz (225 g)	2–3 minutes	Time will depend on type, and whether whole or sliced. Stir or shake gently during cooking.
Onions	Peel, and slice or leave whole. Add only 4 Tbsp (60 ml) water to whole onions.	8 oz (225 g) sliced 6 oz (175 g) whole	4–6 minutes 10–12 minutes	Stir or shake sliced onions and re-arrange whole onions during cooking.
Parsnips	Peel, remove hard core and cut into quarters or halves, depending on size and shape. Place thinner parts toward center. Add dab of butter and 1 Tbsp (15 ml) lemon juice with $\frac{2}{3}$ cup (150 ml) water.	1 lb (450 g)	10–16 minutes	Turn dish during cooking and re-arrange.
Peas	Shell.	1 lb (450 g)	9–11 minutes	Time will vary with the age of the peas. Stir or shake during cooking.
Potatoes Baked	Wash and prick skin with fork. Place on absorbent kitchen paper or napkin. When cooking more than 2 at a time, arrange in a circle.	1 × 6 oz (175 g) potato 2 × 6 oz (175 g) potatoes 4 × 6 oz (175 g) potatoes	4 minutes 6–8 minutes 12–14 minutes	Turn over half-way through cooking period.
Boiled (old)	Wash and peel. Cut into 1-inch (40-g) pieces. Add $\frac{2}{3}$ cup (150 ml) water.	1 lb (450 g)	7–10 minutes	Stir or shake during cooking period. Do not overcook or new potatoes become spongy.
Boiled (new)	Wash and scrub.	1 lb (450 g)	6–8 minutes	
Sweet	Wash and prick skin with fork. Place on paper towels. Use even-sized potatoes.	1 lb (450 g)	5 minutes	Turn over halfway through cooking period.
Spinach	Wash, remove wilted leaves and any tough stems. Do not add water. Best cooked in roasting bag.	1 lb (450 g)	6–7 minutes 5–5$\frac{1}{2}$ minutes	Turn dish during cooking.
Swede/turnip	Peel and dice.	1 lb (450 g)	10–15 minutes	Time will vary with age and quality. Stir or shake during cooking. Mash after standing.
Zucchini	Wash, dry and slice. Do not peel. Do not add more than 2 Tbsp (30 ml) water.	1 lb (450 g)	8–12 minutes	Stir or shake gently twice during cooking. Stand for 2 minutes before draining.

Dried Herbs

Fresh herbs can be dried in the microwave oven and you will find the color and the bouquet are superb. There is a substantial loss of weight when drying herbs so you may like to start off with quite a large quantity. For example 7 oz (200 g) parsley will weigh about $5\frac{3}{4}$ oz (160 g) after the stalks are removed and the weight will be only $\frac{1}{2}$ oz (15 g) after drying. Store your dried herbs in small screw top jars in a cool, dark cupboard.

Dried Parsley
Chop the parsley finely before drying. Put $\frac{1}{2}$ cup (50 g) chopped fresh parsley on a piece of paper towel, place in the microwave oven and microwave on HIGH for 5 minutes or until the parsley and the paper are dry. Stir the parsley several times during cooking (you will find this easier to do with your fingers than with a spoon or fork, as this does not disturb the paper).

Dried Rosemary
Remove the leaves from the stalk before drying. Put $\frac{1}{4}$ cup (25 g) rosemary leaves on a piece of paper towel and microwave on HIGH for 2–2$\frac{1}{2}$ minutes or until the leaves are dry. Stir occasionally during cooking. When the leaves are dry, chop in a food processor or blender.

Dried Basil
Place $\frac{1}{4}$ cup (25 g) basil leaves on a piece of paper towel and microwave on HIGH for 2$\frac{1}{2}$ minutes, stirring occasionally during drying until the leaves are brittle. Do not overcook as basil leaves tend to burn. When the leaves are dry, chop in a food processor or blender.

Fresh Coriander
Put the coriander sprigs on a piece of absorbent kitchen paper and microwave on HIGH for 1$\frac{1}{2}$ minutes or until dry. Remove the stalks and crush the dried leaves between paper towels.

Okra and Tomato Casserole

8 oz (225 g) okra
14-oz (397-g) can tomatoes
salt and freshly ground pepper
1 beef bouillon cube, crumbled
3 sprigs fresh thyme

1
Wash, top and tail the okra and put in a deep casserole with the tomatoes and their juice.

2
Season with salt and pepper and stir in the bouillon cube and the sprigs of thyme.

3
Three-quarters cover with plastic wrap and microwave on HIGH for 12 minutes or until the okra is tender. Stir once or twice during cooking. Remove the sprigs of thyme just before serving.

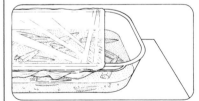

Serves 4.

Eggplant and Butter Bean Casserole

1 lb (450 g) eggplant
salt and freshly ground pepper
1 medium onion, peeled and finely chopped
$\frac{1}{4}$ cup (50 g) butter or margarine
1 level Tbsp (15 ml) cornstarch
1$\frac{1}{4}$ cups (300 ml) tomato juice
$\frac{1}{2}$ beef bouillon cube, crumbled
2 tsp (10 ml) chopped fresh parsley
7$\frac{1}{2}$-oz (213-g) can butter beans, drained

1
Cut off the tops and slice the eggplant into $\frac{1}{2}$-inch (1-cm) slices, then quarter each slice. Sprinkle liberally with salt and leave for 30 minutes. Rinse thoroughly and pat dry with paper towels.

2
Put the onion and butter in a 9-inch (23-cm) round shallow dish and microwave on HIGH for 6 minutes or until the onion begins to brown.

3
Stir in the eggplant and three-quarters cover with plastic wrap. Microwave on HIGH for 6 minutes, stirring twice during cooking.

4
Blend the cornstarch with the tomato juice and stir in the bouillon cube and parsley (the cube will not dissolve at this stage). Pour into the eggplant mixture and add the butter beans.

5
Mix the ingredients well together. Then microwave on HIGH for 7 minutes or until the sauce thickens and the eggplant is soft. Stir twice during cooking. Season to taste.

Serves 3 as a supper dish; 4 as a vegetable accompaniment.

Creamed Mushrooms and Shrimp

1 lb (450 g) button mushrooms, wiped
3 Tbsp (40 g) butter or margarine
2 level Tbsp (30 ml) all-purpose flour
salt and freshly ground pepper
$\frac{1}{2}$-1 level tsp (2.5–5 ml) dried rosemary, well crushed
$\frac{2}{3}$ cup (150 ml) heavy cream
4 oz (100 g) cooked peeled shrimp, thawed and well drained
1 Tbsp (15 ml) lemon juice
whole shrimp for garnish

1

Cut the mushroom stalks level with the caps. Cut larger mushrooms into quarters.

2

Put the butter in a 3-quart (2.8-liter) ovenproof glass mixing bowl and microwave on HIGH for 45 seconds or until melted.

3

Add the mushrooms and stir well so that they are coated with the butter. Without covering, microwave on HIGH for 6 minutes or until the mushrooms are partially cooked and some liquid gathers in the bottom of the bowl. Stir occasionally during cooking.

4

Stir in the flour, then add salt, pepper and herbs to taste. Stir in the cream. Microwave on HIGH for 3 minutes or until the sauce is boiling rapidly, stirring once.

5

Taste the sauce and adjust the seasoning, then stir in the shrimp. Microwave on HIGH for 2 minutes or until the shrimp are heated through. Stir in the lemon juice. Serve hot in individual dishes; garnish with shrimp.

Serves 6 as a starter.

Horsham Mushrooms

16 open flat mushrooms, 2–2$\frac{1}{2}$ inches (5–6 cm) diameter
2 firm tomatoes
8 small bay leaves
salt and freshly ground pepper
1 Tbsp (15 g) butter or margarine

For the sauce
2 level tsp (10 ml) all-purpose flour
1 Tbsp (15 g) butter or margarine, softened
4 Tbsp (60 ml) light cream
2 tsp (10 ml) sherry
1–2 Tbsp (15–30 ml) milk, if needed

1

Cut the stalks level with the mushroom caps. (Discard the stalks or reserve for use in other dishes.) Remove a thin sliver from the top and bottom of the tomatoes and cut each tomato into 4 slices.

2

Arrange half the mushroom caps stalk-side up in a large shallow dish. Cover each cap with a tomato slice and a bay leaf leaving the stalk of the bay leaf protruding. Season with salt and pepper. Top with the remaining mushroom caps, stalk-side down, and dot with butter.

3

Cover and microwave on HIGH for 6 minutes or until the mushrooms are just tender. Reposition the mushrooms and give the dish a half-turn once during cooking.

4

Remove the mushroom sandwiches carefully with a slotted spoon and arrange on a warm dish; carefully remove the bay leaves. Cover and keep warm while making the cream sauce.

5

To complete the sauce, blend the flour and butter together to a soft paste and add to the juices remaining in the cooking dish. Stir thoroughly. Microwave on HIGH for 1 minute or until the sauce thickens, stirring occasionally.

6

Stir in the cream. Add any extra juices given off by the mushrooms, the sherry and the milk if the sauce is too thick. Microwave on LOW for 2 minutes.

7

Replace the mushrooms in the sauce or pour the sauce over the mushrooms on the warm dish. If too thick, thin with a little extra cream.

Serves 4 as an accompanying vegetable or as a starter.

Beans in Sour Cream Sauce

12 oz (350 g) frozen or fresh
  sliced green beans
1 small onion, peeled and finely
  chopped
1 Tbsp (15 g) butter or
  margarine
$\frac{1}{2}$ tsp (2.5 ml) lemon juice
salt and freshly ground pepper
pinch of sugar
8-oz (227-g) can water
  chestnuts, drained and
  chopped
2 Tbsp (30 ml) sour cream or
  plain yogurt

1

Cook the beans according to the
chart on page 76.

2

Combine the onion and butter in a
medium casserole and microwave
on HIGH for 3 minutes or until the
onion softens.

3

Add the lemon juice, salt, pepper
and sugar and microwave on HIGH
for 1 minute. Stir thoroughly.

4

Mix in the beans and water
chestnuts. Cover and microwave
on HIGH for 2 minutes or until the
beans are hot. Stir once during
reheating.

5

Mix in the sour cream, reduce
the setting and microwave on
LOW for 2 minutes, stirring twice
during cooking. Serve hot or cold.

Serves 4.

Variation Use frozen peas and
corn instead of the beans and
water chestnuts.

Stuffed Onions

four 8-oz (225-g) Spanish
  onions, peeled
4 oz (100 g) bacon, preferably
  unsmoked
5 oz (150 g) lean ground beef
2 sprigs parsley
1 clove garlic, peeled and
  crushed (optional)
salt and freshly ground pepper
1 Tbsp (15 ml) bottled fruit
  sauce
1 egg, beaten
micro-fried breadcrumbs to
  garnish (see **Kidneys in
  Madeira, page 57**)

1

Remove a $\frac{1}{2}$-inch (1-cm) slice from
the stalk end of each onion and
trim the base so that the onions
will stand level.

2

Put the onions in a shallow dish.
Cover and microwave on HIGH for
10 minutes or until the outsides
yield to pressure. Leave to cool.

3

Using a grapefruit knife or spoon,
scoop out the centers of the
onions, leaving a sturdy shell.

4

Mince together the bacon, beef,
parsley, garlic and half the
scooped-out onion. Season with
salt and pepper, mix in the sauce
and bind with the egg.

5

Press the stuffing into the onion
cavities. Replace the stuffed onions
in the dish. Do not drain the
cooking juices. Cover tightly and
microwave on HIGH for 8 minutes
or until the meat filling is cooked.
Give the dish a quarter-turn three
times during cooking. Leave to
stand for 5 minutes before
removing the cover. Sprinkle
onions with breadcrumbs. Use up
cooked chopped onions in soup.

Serves 4.

Lyonnaise Potatoes

1 medium onion, peeled and
  finely chopped
1$\frac{1}{2}$ Tbsp (20 g) butter or
  margarine
4 Tbsp (60 ml) heavy cream
1 lb (450 g) mature potatoes,
  peeled and thinly sliced
salt and freshly ground pepper

1

Put the onion and butter in a
9-inch (23-cm) round shallow,
flameproof dish and microwave on
HIGH for 3 minutes or until the
onion is soft. Stir once during
cooking.

2

Stir in the cream, then add the
potatoes, season well with salt and
pepper and toss so that all the
potato slices are well coated with
the butter.

3

Cover the dish with plastic wrap,
pulling back one corner to vent,
and microwave on HIGH for 12
minutes or until the potatoes are
tender. Give the dish a half-turn
once during cooking.

4

Leave to stand for 5 minutes, then
carefully remove the wrap. Brown
the top of the potatoes under the
broiler.

Serves 4.

**Lyonnaise Potatoes, Stuffed
Peppers and Beans in Sour
Cream Sauce (pages 80–1)**

Stuffed Peppers

1 small onion, peeled and
    chopped
1 Tbsp (15 ml) vegetable oil
4 green or red peppers
8 oz (225 g) cooked rice (about
    2 cups)
2 medium tomatoes, peeled
    and chopped
$\frac{1}{4}$ cup (25 g) pinenuts, grated
$\frac{1}{4}$ cup (25 g) currants
2 Tbsp (30 ml) chopped fresh
    parsley
1 level tsp (5 ml) dried dill weed
4 oz (100 g) cooked ground lamb
salt and freshly ground pepper

1

Put the onion and oil in a 9-inch
(23-cm) shallow ovenproof dish and
microwave on HIGH for 3 minutes.
Transfer onion to a bowl.

2

Remove the cores from the
peppers. Cut in half lengthwise and
remove any further seeds. Put the
peppers in the dish with 4 Tbsp
(60 ml) water. Cover with a lid and
microwave on HIGH for 6 minutes,
repositioning the peppers three
times during cooking. Leave
covered while preparing the filling.

3

To complete the filling, mix
remaining ingredients with the
onion, seasoning with salt and
freshly ground pepper to taste.

4

Remove the lid from the peppers
and drain away most of the water,
but do not wipe out the dish.

5

Stuff the peppers with the filling
and arrange in 2 layers in the dish,
separating the layers with a piece
of plastic wrap.

6

Replace the lid and microwave on
LOW for 10 minutes or until the
peppers are cooked and the filling
thoroughly reheated. Give the dish
a quarter-turn three times during
the cooking period.

7

Serve the top 4 peppers first, then
remove the plastic wrap before
serving the remainder. Serve with
Tomato Sauce (see page 94).

Serves 4.

Quick Sautéed Vegetables
(page 83) in a Corningware
browning dish

Colcannon

1 lb (450 g) potatoes, peeled
1 lb (450 g) cabbage, shredded
$\frac{2}{3}$ cup (150 ml) heavy cream
salt and freshly ground pepper
2 oz (50 g) Cheddar cheese,
    grated

1

Cut up the potatoes into even-
sized pieces and place in a roasting
bag with $\frac{2}{3}$ cup (150 ml) water.
Seal loosely with a non-metallic
fastening such as an elastic band.

2

Cook on HIGH for 7–10 minutes
until tender. Carefully remove the
potatoes from the roasting bag and
transfer to a large bowl and mash
well.

3

Place the cabbage in the roasting
bag and seal as above. Cook on
HIGH for 9–11 minutes until
tender. Drain well and add to the
mashed potato.

4

Mix in the cream and plenty of
seasoning and turn into an
ovenproof serving dish. Sprinkle
with cheese.

5

Without covering, microwave on
HIGH for 5 minutes or until
thoroughly reheated. Stir
occasionally during cooking.
Brown under the broiler if wished,
to give a golden topping.

Serves 4.

Soft Sautéed Potatoes

2 Tbsp (25 g) butter or
  margarine
1½ lb (700 g) peeled potatoes, cut
  into 1½-inch (4-cm) chunks
1 level Tbsp (15 ml) flour
  seasoned with paprika

1

Preheat a large browning dish to
maximum according to the
manufacturer's instructions,
adding the butter during the last
30 seconds. While the browning
dish is heating toss the potatoes in
the seasoned flour.

2

When the browning dish is ready
and the butter sizzling, toss in the
potatoes and microwave on HIGH
for 1 minute. Quickly turn the
potatoes over and microwave on
HIGH for a further minute.

3

Reposition the potatoes, cover
with the lid and microwave on
HIGH for 5 minutes, stirring and
repositioning the potatoes once
during cooking. Test by piercing
with a fork. The potatoes should be
almost tender.

4

Leave covered with the lid for 5
minutes before serving. (The
potatoes will continue cooking
during this time.)

Serves 4.

Ratatouille

12 oz (350 g) eggplant, cut into
  small chunks
salt and freshly ground pepper
2 Tbsp (30 ml) vegetable oil
2 medium onions, peeled and
  finely chopped
4 medium tomatoes, peeled
  and chopped
½ small red pepper, seeded and
  thinly sliced
½ small green pepper, seeded
  and thinly sliced
2 medium zucchini, thinly
  sliced
1 clove garlic, peeled and
  crushed
2 Tbsp (30 ml) tomato paste

1

Cut off the tops and slice the
eggplant thickly. Cut into chunky
pieces and place in a bowl.
Sprinkle with salt and leave for 30
minutes. Drain and pat dry with
paper towels.

2

Put the oil and onions in a
3-quart (2.8-liter) ovenproof glass
bowl and microwave on HIGH for
3 minutes until the onion softens.

3

Stir in the remaining vegetables,
garlic and tomato paste and mix
well. Three-quarters cover with
plastic wrap and microwave on
HIGH for 18 minutes or until the
vegetables are tender. Stir two or
three times during cooking.

4

Season to taste. Serve hot as an
accompaniment to broiled meats
or cold as a starter, with crusty
French bread.

Serves 4.

Creamed Spinach

1 lb (450 g) fresh spinach
2 Tbsp (25 g) butter or
  margarine
⅔ cup (150 ml) light cream
¼ level tsp (1.25 ml) ground
  nutmeg
salt and freshly ground pepper

1

Wash the spinach leaves in plenty
of cold water and remove any
coarse stems. Place the leaves in a
large roasting bag and close loosely
with an elastic band.

2

Place the bag upright on the oven
shelf and microwave on HIGH for 6
minutes or until the spinach is
packed down and cooked.

3

Carefully open the bag and tip the
contents into a sieve. Push down
with a wooden spoon to remove
excess moisture, and chop the
spinach roughly.

4

Put the butter and light cream in
a 1½-quart (1.1-liter) bowl and
microwave on HIGH for 1 minute
to melt the butter. Add the
chopped spinach, nutmeg and salt
and pepper. Reheat to serving
temperature on HIGH for
1½–2 minutes.

Serves 4.

Red Cabbage and Apple Casserole

1 lb (450 g) red cabbage, finely shredded
8 oz (225 g) cooking apple, peeled, cored and sliced
4 Tbsp (60 ml) red wine vinegar
$\frac{1}{4}$ cup (50 g) light brown sugar
2 level tsp (10 ml) Dijon-style mustard
pinch ground cloves
salt and freshly ground pepper

1

Put the shredded cabbage and apple into a 2-quart (2-liter) ovenproof glass casserole and mix together. Add the remaining ingredients and stir in well.

2

Cover the casserole and microwave on HIGH for 15 minutes, or until cooked, stirring three times during cooking. Check seasoning. Serve with pork or game dishes.

Serves 4.

Quick Sautéed Vegetables

1 Tbsp (15 g) butter or margarine
$\frac{1}{2}$ red, yellow or green pepper, seeded and sliced
1 zucchini, thinly sliced
2 oz (50 g) mushrooms, wiped and sliced
3 oz (75 g) broccoli florets
2 oz (50 g) spring onions, trimmed and finely sliced
salt and freshly ground pepper
soy sauce (optional)

1

Preheat the browning dish to maximum according to manufacturer's instructions, adding the butter during the last 30 seconds.

2

Add all the vegetables quickly to the sizzling butter and stir to coat. Microwave on HIGH for 2 minutes until the vegetables are slightly softened. Season well with salt and pepper and soy sauce to taste; serve hot.

Serves 2.

Note Vary the vegetables according to taste—use red pepper slices, carrot sticks, celery and fennel slices. Serve with soy sauce, if wished.

Curried Lentils

2 Tbsp (30 ml) vegetable oil
1 medium onion, peeled and very finely chopped
1 clove garlic, peeled and crushed
1 level Tbsp (15 ml) mild curry paste
6 oz (175 g) red lentils, rinsed and drained
1 level tsp (5 ml) salt

1

Put the oil in a 3-quart (2.8-liter) ovenproof glass bowl and stir in the onion and garlic. Microwave on HIGH for 3 minutes or until the onion is soft. Stir occasionally during cooking.

2

Stir in the curry paste and lentils and microwave on HIGH for 3 minutes, stirring occasionally.

3

Add the salt and $4\frac{1}{2}$ cups (1 liter) boiling water and stir thoroughly. Microwave on HIGH for 25 minutes or until the lentils are just tender, stirring occasionally during cooking.

4

Mash thoroughly or purée the lentils in a blender. Serve hot.

Serves 4.

Note Curry paste is easy to use but if you do not have it substitute 1 level Tbsp (15 ml) curry powder.

CHAPTER SEVEN

Pasta, Rice and Grains

Cooking pasta

Because pasta is a dried product, it must be cooked in a considerable quantity of water and it must have sufficient time to absorb this water. There is therefore no saving in time when you cook pasta by microwave. On the other hand, the results are good and you may often find it convenient. It is also a much cleaner process than the conventional method—there is no contact between the bottom of the bowl and a direct heating element so that the pasta cannot stick on the bottom. To be sure that the pasta pieces do not stick together, add a little vegetable oil to the cooking water.

To cook pasta by microwave, the water must be fully boiling when the pasta is put in; it will then stay hot enough for cooking. Smaller pieces of pasta such as shells, elbow macaroni or spaghetti can be added all at once to the boiling water but larger pieces like lasagne must be added in two batches, bringing the water back to the boil after each batch of leaves is lowered in. If lasagne is not treated this way it will stick together as a solid mass.

Cooking times vary depending on the variety of the pasta. All dried pasta requires the same amount of cooking time but the standing time will vary.

Noodles require practically no standing time at all. Freshly made pasta, whether home-made or commercially prepared, is much softer than the dry, brittle type that we are accustomed to using and it is usually made with eggs rather than simply durum flour and water. It requires practically no cooking. Microwave this type of pasta for only 1 minute and do not give it a standing time, but drain and serve at once.

Cooked pasta can be reheated on HIGH unless mixed with a sauce that would be better reheated on LOW; cover while reheating. It can also be frozen and reheated in the microwave oven and, if you intend to do this, it is best to arrange it in a circle in the dish before freezing. It will not save any time to freeze and reheat, as it takes just as long to thaw and reheat as to cook from fresh, but it is a useful standby for other members of the household who may be either unwilling or unable to cook.

When reheating pasta in a sauce, either mix the sauce thoroughly with the pasta before freezing or arrange the pasta round the outside of the dish and the sauce in the middle.

Cooking rice

As for pasta, cooking rice by microwave saves no time over conventional methods. But the results are so good, with each grain tender and separate, that you may well prefer it.

The amount of rice that you can cook at any one time is in direct relation to the size of the container you use. You can cook about 1 lb (450 g) in a 3-quart (2.8-liter) ovenproof glass bowl or similar container. Traditional long-grain rice can be cooked by the old-fashioned method of using lots and lots of boiling salted water; cook the rice uncovered, then pour into a colander, rinse and leave to drain. Or use the measured amount of water and salt recommended on the packet; it is usual to use double the volume of water to rice, add a measured amount of salt and cook, covered, until tender.

So many different kinds of rice are now obtainable that it is difficult to give precise recommendations for cooking times but I find that easy-cook rice takes just about the same length of time as untreated rice. The more pre-cooking that has taken place in manufacture, the less cooking time will be needed. Pudding rice is more difficult to tenderize, and when it is cooked in milk it is likely to boil over. If your microwave oven is fitted with a probe you can avoid this. In other cases either cook the rice in water before adding milk (evaporated is best for this because it is concentrated), or cook on a LOW setting. Cook brown rice in the same way as white rice but allow a longer cooking time.

Frozen rice thaws and heats very quickly. When reheating, add 1–2 tsp (5–10 ml) water so that a little steam is created and microwave on HIGH, breaking up the lumps as soon as it is possible. It is best to reheat uncovered to prevent overcooking.

To give extra flavor to boiled rice add a bouillon cube to the cooking water or cook the rice completely in freshly made stock.

Cooking Noodles

8 oz (225 g) pasta shapes, such
   as tagliatelle, spaghetti,
   macaroni
2 level tsp (10 ml) salt
1 tsp (5 ml) vegetable oil

1

Boil 2 quarts (2 liters) water in a
kettle and pour into a deep
casserole or 3-quart (2.8-liter)
ovenproof glass bowl. Add the salt
and the oil.

2

Bring the water back to a full
rolling boil in the microwave oven
set on HIGH. Quickly lower in the
pasta and without covering,
microwave on HIGH for 5 minutes
until partially cooked.

3

Remove from the oven, stir and
cover. Leave to stand for 2–5
minutes until the pasta is firm to
the bite. (Standing times vary
according to the type of pasta; eg,
stand tagliatelle for 2 minutes,
spaghetti and macaroni for 5
minutes.) Drain and serve.

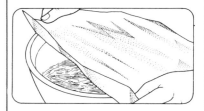

Serves 4.

Spaghetti Bolognese

$2\frac{1}{4}$ cups (450 ml) Bolognese
   Sauce (see page 94)
8 oz (225 g) spaghetti

1

Prepare and cook the sauce.

2

Cook the spaghetti as directed left.
Leave to stand.

3

During the standing time, reheat
the sauce if necessary. Drain the
spaghetti and serve with the sauce.

Serves 4.

Spaghetti Napolitana

$2\frac{1}{4}$ cups (450 ml) Tomato Sauce
   (see page 94)
8 oz (225 g) spaghetti

1

Prepare and cook the sauce.

2

Cook the spaghetti as directed left.
Leave to stand.

3

During the standing time, reheat
the sauce if necessary. Drain the
spaghetti and serve with the sauce.

Serves 4.

Macaroni and Cheese

2¼ cups (450 ml) Cheese Sauce
   (see page 92)
6 oz (175 g) macaroni
4 Tbsp (175 g) milk
2 oz (50 g) Cheddar cheese,
   grated

1

Prepare and cook the sauce. Cover and set aside while preparing the pasta.

2

Cook the macaroni as directed on page 84.

3

Drain the macaroni and return to the casserole, bowl or an ovenproof serving dish. Stir the sauce and milk.

4

Sprinkle with the cheese, cover and microwave on LOW until reheated. Brown under the broiler if wished, to give a golden topping.

Serves 4.

Noodles with Shrimp Sauce

1¼ cups (300 ml) Shrimp Sauce
   (see page 94)
8 oz (225 g) noodles

1

Prepare and cook the sauce. Cover and set aside while preparing the pasta.

2

Cook the noodles as directed on page 84.

3

Reheat the sauce, if necessary. Drain the noodles and serve with the sauce.

Serves 4.

Tagliatelle with Walnut and Spinach Sauce

1 recipe Walnut and Spinach
   Sauce (see page 95)
4 oz (125 g) tagliatelle or other
   pasta

1

Prepare and cook the sauce. Cover and set aside while preparing the pasta.

2

Cook the pasta as directed on page 84. Leave to stand.

3

During the standing time, reheat the sauce if necessary. Drain the pasta and serve with the sauce. Top with Parmesan cheese.

Serves 2.

Crispy-topped Creamed Spaghetti

4 strips bacon, finely chopped
½ cup (40 g) fresh dark
   breadcrumbs
1 Tbsp (15 g) butter
¼ cup (50 g) butter or
   margarine
1 small onion, peeled and finely
   chopped
2 Tbsp (25 g) all-purpose flour
salt and freshly ground pepper
⅔ cup (150 ml) heavy cream
1½ cups (350 ml) milk
6 oz (175 g) Cheddar cheese,
   grated
6 oz (175 g) spaghetti, freshly
   cooked

1

First make the topping. Mix the bacon and breadcrumbs together in a large ovenproof glass bowl. Add the butter and microwave on HIGH for 4 minutes or until the bacon is crisp and the crumbs are golden brown and have absorbed all of the bacon fat. Stir occasionally during cooking. Turn out on to a plate and set aside.

2

Using the same bowl, put in the butter and onion. Microwave on HIGH for 3 minutes or until the onion is soft, stirring once.

3

Stir in the flour, salt and pepper. Then add the cream and milk. Stir thoroughly. Microwave on HIGH for 4½ minutes or until the sauce has thickened. Beat after each minute with a balloon whisk.

4

Stir the cheese into the sauce. Mix in the spaghetti and microwave on HIGH for 1 minute or until thoroughly reheated.

5

Turn the creamed spaghetti into a warmed serving dish and sprinkle the crispy bacon crumbs on top.

Serves 4.

Boiled Rice

2 cups (450 g) long-grain rice
4 level tsp (20 ml) salt

1

Rinse the rice and put in a 3-quart (2.8-liter) ovenproof glass bowl with 2 quarts (2 liters) boiling water and the salt. Stir once.

2

Without covering, microwave on HIGH for 15 minutes or until a grain of rice can be broken when pressed with a fork. Stir once during cooking. Cover and leave to stand for 5 minutes. Drain through a colander under hot running water. If rice is to be served cold, drain under cold running water.

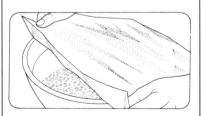

Serves 6.

Saffron Rice
To color rice yellow, add a small pinch of saffron to the rice and water in Step 1.

Boiled Rice All-in-one Method

1¼ cups (275 g) long-grain rice
1½ level tsp (7.5 ml) salt

1

Put the rice, salt and 3¼ cups (750 ml) boiling water in a large casserole, stir once, then cover with a lid.

2

Microwave on HIGH for about 15 minutes or until a grain of rice can be broken easily with the side of a fork. (Most of the water should have been absorbed. If the rice is dry but not quite cooked add 1–2 Tbsp (15–30 ml) boiling water.)

3

Leave to stand, covered, for 8 minutes, by which time all the water should be absorbed and the rice tender.

Serves 4.

Note Various kinds of rice absorb different amounts of liquid, but as a rule put into a bowl the required quantity of rice and double the volume in water, adding salt to taste. For exact instructions follow the recommendations on the package but add a few extra tablespoons of water.

Boiled Brown Rice

½ cup (100 g) brown rice
½ level tsp (2.5 ml) salt
boiling water

1

Put the rice, salt and 2½ cups (600 ml) boiling water in a medium casserole. Stir once.

2

Cover with the lid and microwave on HIGH for 30 minutes or until the rice is nearly cooked and most of the water absorbed. Stir once during cooking.

3

Stir once after cooking, then replace the lid and leave to stand for 5 minutes or until the rice is fully cooked and all the liquid is absorbed. If on the first testing the liquid is absorbed but the rice is not yet cooked, add 5–6 Tbsp (75–90 ml) boiling water.

Serves 2.

Note The volume of rice increases considerably when cooked, be sure to use a casserole that is big enough.

Brown Rice (Old-fashioned Method)

½ cup (100 g) brown rice
½ level tsp (2.5 ml) salt
1 quart (1 liter) boiling water

1

Combine the rice, salt and boiling water in a large ovenproof glass bowl and stir once.

2

Without covering, microwave on HIGH for 30 minutes, stirring occasionally.

3

Drain the rice through a colander, then put into a serving dish and cover. Leave to stand for 5 minutes.

Serves 2.

Note Any remaining droplets of water will be absorbed by the hot rice as it stands.

Chinese Fried Rice

3 Tbsp (40 g) butter or
  margarine
2 Tbsp (30 ml) chopped spring
  onions
6 cups (450 g) cooked long-grain
  rice
2 Tbsp (30 ml) soy sauce
4 oz (100 g) ham, cut into strips
4 eggs
freshly ground pepper

1

Put 2 Tbsp (25 g) butter in a large bowl or suitable serving dish and microwave on HIGH for 45 seconds or until melted.

2

Stir in the spring onions and the rice and microwave on HIGH for 3 minutes or until thoroughly heated. Stir once during cooking.

3

Stir in the soy sauce and ham and microwave on HIGH for 2 minutes or until the mixture is thoroughly hot. Cover tightly while preparing the eggs.

4

Put the remaining 1 Tbsp (15 g) butter in a bowl or cup and microwave on HIGH for 10 seconds or until the butter is very soft. Add the eggs, 4 Tbsp (60 ml) water and a little pepper and beat thoroughly. Microwave on HIGH for 2½ minutes or until the eggs are just set but not completely cooked. Stir the mixture every 30 seconds during cooking, drawing the edges to the middle and making sure that no large lumps are left to set.

5

Stir the egg into the rice mixture and serve at once.

Serves 4–6.

Spicy Pilaff

3 Tbsp (40 g) butter or
  margarine
$\frac{3}{4}$ cup (175 g) long-grain rice,
  rinsed, drained and dried
$\frac{1}{3}$ cup (40 g) mixed nuts, finely
  chopped
2$\frac{1}{4}$ cups (450 ml) hot chicken
  stock
$\frac{1}{2}$ level tsp (2.5 ml) salt
$\frac{1}{2}$ level tsp (2.5 ml) ground
  cardamom
$\frac{1}{2}$ level tsp (2.5 ml) ground
  turmeric
$\frac{1}{4}$ cup (25 g) raisins
$\frac{1}{4}$ red pepper, seeded and diced
4 Tbsp (60 ml) frozen peas

1

Put the butter in a 2-quart (1.7-
liter) casserole and microwave on
HIGH for 45 seconds or until
the butter is melted.

2

Stir in the rice and microwave on
HIGH for 3 minutes, stirring once
during cooking.

3

Add the nuts and microwave on
HIGH for 2 minutes or until the
rice is a pale gold color.

4

Stir in the remaining ingredients
and microwave on HIGH for 12
minutes or until the rice is just
tender and most of the liquid
absorbed. Stir the rice once
during cooking.

5

Stir lightly once again, then cover
tightly and leave for 5 minutes
during which time the liquid
should be absorbed.

6

Fork up the rice, then serve as a
light supper dish or vegetable
accompaniment to a main course.

Serves 3–4.

Barley and Mushroom Casserole

$\frac{1}{4}$ cup (50 g) butter or
  margarine
1 medium onion, peeled and
  finely chopped
$\frac{3}{4}$ cup (175 g) pearl barley
8 oz (225 g) mushrooms, wiped
  and quartered
1 level tsp (5 ml) dried basil
salt and freshly ground pepper

1

Put the butter in a large casserole
and microwave on HIGH for 45
seconds or until melted.

2

Stir in the onion and microwave on
HIGH for 3 minutes or until soft.
Stir once during cooking.

3

Stir in the pearl barley and
microwave on HIGH for 5 minutes
or until a light golden color (you
may see some brown flakes; this is
the onion frying further). Stir
twice during cooking.

4

Add 3$\frac{1}{4}$ cups (750 ml) boiling water
and the mushrooms. Stir in the
basil and season with salt and
pepper. Cover with a lid and
microwave on HIGH for 30
minutes, stirring twice during
cooking. Leave to stand for 10–15
minutes until tender.

*Serves 4–6 as an accompanying
vegetable.*

Oatmeal

1$\frac{2}{3}$ cups (150 g) rolled oats
1 level tsp (5 ml) salt

1

Combine the oats, salt and 3$\frac{3}{4}$ cups
(900 ml) water in a 3-quart (2.8-
liter) ovenproof glass bowl and stir
well. Microwave on HIGH for 5
minutes, stirring once during
cooking. Reduce the setting and
microwave on MEDIUM for 10
minutes or on LOW for 20
minutes, stirring once or twice to
break up any lumps that may form.

2

Stir, then cover and store in a cool
place overnight, if wished.

3

To reheat, three-quarters cover
the bowl with plastic wrap and
microwave on HIGH for 6–8
minutes, stirring two or three
times during reheating. To reheat
a single bowl, microwave on HIGH
for about 1$\frac{1}{2}$ minutes, stirring once
during reheating and once again
before serving.

Serves 6.

Note Most oats are now quick
cooking, made from rolled oats
which have been partially cooked
in manufacture. Oatmeal improves
if made the night before, then
covered to prevent a crust forming
and stored in the refrigerator or
cool place until the next morning.
Thin down the cereal with milk,
cream or water and serve with
sugar or extra salt if preferred.

CHAPTER EIGHT

Sauces

Cooking sauces by microwave is foolproof. Unlike conventional cooking, when the direct contact between the base of the pan and the heat can cause lumps and burning, in the microwave oven the heat is created within the food so these are less likely to occur. All you need is a long-handled wooden spoon, a balloon whisk and a cooking bowl.

Roux-based sauces
Sauces based on a roux—that is, when the flour and butter are cooked together to a paste before the liquid is added—are simply marvellous cooked in a microwave oven. Once you have made a sauce this way you will never do it any other way. This method includes Basic white sauce, Béchamel sauce and many variations.

Brown sauces
You can achieve brown sauces in the microwave oven, too. Use a deep bowl or dish and be sure that your container is made of a material that will withstand the temperature of the very hot fat. Cook the onion in butter or oil until it is brown, then stir in the flour and allow this to cook for a little while before adding further ingredients. Alternatively mix an equal volume of vegetable oil and flour in a deep dish and microwave on HIGH for 5–10 minutes until brown. Add the onion, which will immediately sizzle and brown, and then add hot stock and any other ingredients.

Sauces that are cooked by reduction, such as Tomato sauce, should be cooked uncovered. They must be stirred frequently because the boiling bubbles will burst and splatter as the sauce thickens.

Thickening sauces
Take care when cooking sauces that are thickened with eggs. These are the sauces that are normally cooked in the top half of a double saucepan. Practice cooking these sauces on LOW and you will soon find that you are able to achieve a good result when cooking on HIGH, which will be much quicker. It is imperative to whisk every few seconds and not to overcook.

When cooking sauces thickened with cornstarch or arrowroot and including no butter or eggs, make sure that the starch is blended thoroughly with cold liquid before adding hot liquid. When whisking these sauces the whisk must reach right to the bottom of the bowl.

In meat sauces made with freshly ground meat, either brown the meat conventionally, or in a browning dish, or cook on a roasting rack in a shallow dish so that the fat can be poured off.

Freezing sauces
Most sauces can be made in advance and many can be frozen. But sauces containing cream, sour cream, yogurt or egg must not be boiled. If you intend to reheat these sauces, omit these ingredients and add them after reheating just to boiling point.

White sauces
The basic white sauce is the foundation for any number of variations. It is used as a pouring or coating sauce and when very thick as a panada for soufflés. If a white sauce is not to be served immediately it is better to make it fairly thin because sauces thicken as they cool and during prolonged standing time. The basic white sauce can be made in advance and stored in the refrigerator. Cover the surface of the sauce with a piece of damp waxed paper or plastic wrap to prevent a skin forming on top.

The Basic White Sauce recipe (opposite) freezes well. When cold pour into a rigid container, seal and freeze. Thaw in the microwave oven for about 5 minutes then tip into a larger bowl so that the sauce can be beaten smooth and heated to the required temperature.

Basic White Sauce

1½ Tbsp (20 g) butter or
  margarine
1½ Tbsp (20 g) flour
1¼ cups (300 ml) milk or milk
  and stock
salt and freshly ground black
  pepper

1

Put the butter in a bowl and microwave on HIGH until melted.

2

Stir in the flour and microwave on HIGH for a few seconds to help the flour to cook and avoid an uncooked starchy taste.

3

Gradually mix in the liquid (this is usually milk but it can be milk and stock combined). Microwave on HIGH for the time stated in the chart, then whisk thoroughly with a balloon whisk to prevent lumps forming.

4

Continue microwaving on HIGH, whisking every 30 seconds until the sauce thickens. Thicker sauces cook slightly more quickly than thin sauces. Add seasoning to taste. Add additional ingredients such as parsley, cheese and egg just before serving.

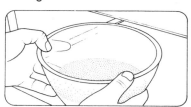

Makes 1¼ cups (300 ml) pouring sauce.

Basic White Sauce

(All microwave cooking on HIGH)

	Butter or margarine Quantity	Time to melt (Step 1)	Flour Quantity	Time to cook mixed with butter (Step 2)	Liquid (cold) Quantity	Time to cook (stirred in gradually) (Step 3)	Final cooking period whisking every 30 seconds (Step 4)
Pouring sauce	1½ Tbsp (20 g)	20 secs	1½ Tbsp (20 g)	20 secs	1¼ cups (300 ml)	1 min	2 mins
	3 Tbsp (40 g)	45 secs	3 Tbsp (40 g)	30 secs	2½ cups (600 ml)	1½ min	3½ mins
Coating sauce	2 Tbsp (25 g)	30 secs	2 Tbsp (25 g)	30 secs	1¼ cups (300 ml)	45 secs	1¾ mins
	¼ cup (50 g)	1 min	¼ cup (50 g)	45 secs	2½ cups (600 ml)	1 min	3 mins
Panada (thick)	2 Tbsp (25 g)	30 secs	2 Tbsp (25 g)	30 secs	⅔ cup (150 ml)	½ min	1 min

Note Allow extra time for larger quantities; eg, 1 quart (1.1 liter) sauce takes 6½ minutes on HIGH. If the liquid is warm when added, reduce the cooking time. White sauce thickens on standing, so it may be necessary to thin it down with a little extra liquid on reheating.

Cheese Sauce

1½ Tbsp (20 g) butter or
   margarine
1½ Tbsp (20 g) flour
1¼ cups (300 ml) milk
4 level Tbsp (60 ml) grated
   cheese (hard cheese is best)
¼ level tsp (1.25 ml) prepared
   mustard
pinch of salt
shake of cayenne pepper

1

Put the butter in a bowl and
microwave on HIGH until melted.

2

Stir in the flour and microwave on
HIGH for a few seconds to help the
flour to cook and avoid an
uncooked starchy taste.

3

Gradually mix in the milk.
Microwave on HIGH for the time
stated in the chart (page 91), then
whisk thoroughly.

4

Continue microwaving on HIGH,
whisking every 30 seconds until
the sauce thickens. Stir in the
grated cheese, mustard, salt and
cayenne pepper. Reheat if
necessary, but do not boil.

*Makes 1¼ cups (300 ml) pouring
sauce.*

Parsley Sauce

1½ Tbsp (20 g) butter or
   margarine
1½ Tbsp (20 g) flour
1¼ cups (300 ml) milk
2 tsp (10 ml) chopped fresh
   parsley
salt and freshly ground pepper

1

Put the butter in a bowl and
microwave on HIGH until melted.

2

Stir in the flour and microwave on
HIGH for a few seconds to help the
flour to cook and avoid an
uncooked starchy taste.

3

Gradually mix in the milk.
Microwave on HIGH for the time
stated in the chart (page 91), then
whisk thoroughly.

4

Continue microwaving on HIGH,
whisking every 30 seconds until
the sauce thickens. Add the parsley
during the last 2 minutes of the
cooking period. Season with salt
and pepper.

*Makes 1¼ cups (300 ml) pouring
sauce.*

Egg Sauce

1½ Tbsp (20 g) butter or
   margarine
1½ Tbsp (20 g) flour
1¼ cups (300 ml) milk
1 hard-boiled egg, chopped
salt and freshly ground pepper

1

Put the butter in a bowl and
microwave on HIGH until melted.

2

Stir in the flour and microwave on
HIGH for a few seconds to help the
flour to cook and avoid an
uncooked starchy taste.

3

Gradually mix in the milk.
Microwave on HIGH for the time
stated in the chart (page 91), then
whisk thoroughly.

4

Continue microwaving on HIGH,
whisking every 30 seconds until
the sauce thickens. Add the hard-
boiled egg during the last 30
seconds of the cooking period.
Season with salt and pepper.

*Makes 1¼ cups (300 ml) pouring
sauce.*

Quick Tomato Sauce

1½ Tbsp (20 g) butter or
   margarine
1½ Tbsp (20 g) flour
⅔ cup (150 ml) milk
⅔ cup (150 ml) chicken stock
4 Tbsp (60 ml) tomato ketchup
salt and freshly ground pepper

1

Put the butter in a bowl and
microwave on HIGH until melted.

2

Stir in the flour and microwave on
HIGH for a few seconds to help the
flour to cook and avoid an
uncooked starchy taste.

3

Gradually mix in the milk and
stock combined. Microwave on
HIGH for the time stated in the
chart (page 91), then whisk
thoroughly.

4

Continue microwaving on HIGH,
whisking every 30 seconds until
the sauce thickens. Add the tomato
ketchup and microwave for 1
minute more. Season with salt and
pepper.

*Makes 1¼ cups (300 ml) pouring
sauce.*

Béchamel Sauce

1¼ cups (300 ml) milk
1 bay leaf
1 thyme sprig
1 parsley sprig, roughly
   chopped
¼ level tsp (1.25 ml) grated
   nutmeg
small piece onion
small piece carrot
2 Tbsp (25 g) butter
2 Tbsp (25 g) all-purpose flour
salt and freshly ground pepper

1

Put the milk in a large cup. Add
the herbs, nutmeg and vegetables.
Without covering, microwave on
HIGH for 1½ minutes or until the
milk begins to steam.

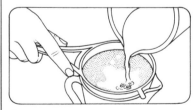

2

Cover the cup and set aside for
15–30 minutes (the longer you
leave it the better the flavor of the
sauce will be). Strain the milk into
a large cup or lipped bowl.

3

Put the butter in a medium bowl
and microwave on HIGH for 30
seconds or until melted.

4

Stir in the flour and microwave on
HIGH for 20 seconds or until the
mixture puffs up slightly.

5

Gradually add the infused milk
to the roux mixture, beating
vigorously with a balloon whisk.
Microwave on HIGH for 2 minutes
or until the sauce thickens. Whisk
frequently during cooking. Season
to taste with salt and freshly
ground black pepper.

*Makes 1¼ cups (300 ml) coating
sauce.*

Note To make a pouring sauce,
double the quantity of milk. To
make a thick sauce for use in hot
soufflés, halve the quantity of milk.

Tomato Sauce

2 Tbsp butter or margarine
1 medium onion, peeled and
  finely chopped
1 clove garlic, peeled and
  crushed
14-oz (397-g) can tomatoes
2 Tbsp (30 ml) tomato paste
1 level tsp (5 ml) dried basil
pinch of sugar
salt and freshly ground pepper
1 level Tbsp (15 ml) arrowroot
  or cornstarch
3 Tbsp (45 ml) red wine

1

In a 3-quart (2.8-liter) ovenproof
glass bowl, heat the butter on
HIGH for 15 seconds or until
melted. Stir in the onion and garlic
and microwave on HIGH for 6
minutes or until the onion starts to
brown.

2

Add the tomatoes, 1¼ cups (300 ml)
water, tomato paste, basil, sugar
and seasoning and microwave on
HIGH for 15 minutes or until the
sauce reduces and thickens. Stir
occasionally during cooking.

3

Blend the arrowroot with the
wine, pour into the sauce and
microwave on HIGH for 3 minutes
until boiling. Stir every minute
during cooking.

4

Allow to cool for about 10 minutes
then purée in a blender. Adjust the
seasoning to taste.

5

To reheat, three-quarters cover
with plastic wrap and microwave
on HIGH to serving temperature.

Makes about 2½ cups (600 ml).

Shrimp Sauce

1 tsp (5 ml) olive oil
1 small clove garlic, peeled and
  crushed
6 Tbsp (100 ml) tomato juice
¼ cup (50 ml) tomato paste
3 Tbsp (45 ml) red wine
1 Tbsp (15 ml) chopped parsley
½ level tsp (2.5 ml) sugar
½ level tsp (2.5 ml) dried
  tarragon
¼ level tsp (1.25 ml) salt
¼ level tsp (1.25 ml) freshly
  ground black pepper
8 oz (225 g) cooked shelled
  shrimp

1

Put all the ingredients, except
the shrimp, in a medium
ovenproof glass bowl or a
casserole. Stir well, then
microwave on HIGH for 5 minutes
or until the sauce is bubbling
around the edges. Stir once, then
microwave on HIGH for a further
2 minutes.

2

Stir in the shrimp. Three-quarters
cover with plastic wrap, and
microwave on HIGH for 3 minutes
or until the shrimp are fully
heated. Stir once during cooking.

Makes about 2 cups (450 ml).

Bolognese Sauce

1 medium onion, peeled and
  very finely chopped
2 Tbsp (30 ml) olive oil
8 oz (225 g) fresh ground lamb
  or beef
½ level tsp (2.5 ml) ground bay
  leaves
½ level tsp (2.5 ml) dried basil
1 level tsp (5 ml) dried parsley
salt and freshly ground black
  pepper
3 Tbsp (45 ml) red wine
1 Tbsp (15 ml) tomato paste
14-oz (397-g) can tomatoes,
  crushed with their juice

1

Combine the onion and oil in a
3-quart (2.8-liter) ovenproof glass
bowl and microwave on HIGH for
7 minutes or until the onion is
browned. Stir occasionally during
cooking.

2

Stir in the meat and microwave on
HIGH for 5 minutes, stirring once
during cooking.

3

Add the herbs, seasoning, wine,
tomato paste and the tomatoes.
Stir thoroughly so that no lumps
of meat are sticking together and
microwave on HIGH for 10
minutes or until the sauce is thick.
Stir occasionally during cooking.

Enough for 3–4 servings of pasta.

Note Fresh ripe tomatoes can be
used when they are in season. You
will require about 2 lb (900 g). The
tomatoes should be skinned and
chopped.

Walnut and Spinach Sauce

4 oz (100 g) bacon, chopped
1 Tbsp (15 ml) vegetable oil
1 medium onion, peeled and
   finely chopped
1 clove garlic, peeled and
   crushed
1 lb (450 g) fresh spinach,
   cooked and chopped, or 10-oz
   (283-g) package frozen
   chopped spinach, thawed and
   drained
⅔ cup (150 ml) light cream
2 oz (50 g) shelled walnuts,
   coarsely chopped
1 oz (25 g) Parmesan cheese,
   grated

1

In a 1½-quart (1.5-liter) ovenproof pan or bowl microwave the bacon and oil on HIGH for 2 minutes or until cooked, covered with a piece of paper towel to minimize splattering.

2

Stir in the onion and garlic. Microwave uncovered on HIGH for 2 minutes until soft. Stir in the spinach and cream and continue to microwave on HIGH for 5 minutes or until well heated, stirring halfway through cooking time. Stir in the walnuts.

Serves 2 as a main dish with freshly cooked pasta or rice and top with Parmesan cheese.

Rich Brown Sauce

5 Tbsp (75 ml) vegetable oil
¼ cup (50 g) all-purpose flour
1 large onion, peeled and finely
   chopped
1 clove garlic, peeled and
   crushed
2 celery stalks, finely chopped
2 strips bacon, finely chopped
1 medium carrot, peeled and
   grated

1

Blend the oil and flour together in a large deep casserole or 3-quart (2.8-liter) bowl. Microwave on HIGH for 7 minutes or until fudge colored. Stir once during cooking (the flour and oil will appear sandy and rough).

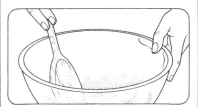

2

Stir in the onion and garlic and microwave on HIGH for 3 minutes. Add the celery, bacon and carrot and microwave on HIGH for 2 minutes.

3

Add the remaining ingredients, three-quarters cover with plastic wrap and microwave on HIGH for 20 minutes or until the sauce has thickened. Stir occasionally during cooking.

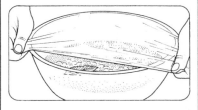

4

Remove the bay leaf, allow to cool a little and purée the sauce in a blender. Adjust the seasoning. Reheat if necessary.

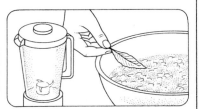

Makes 3¾ cups (900 ml).

Note This sauce is good with many meat dishes and can be added to soups for extra flavor. The sauce thickens considerably as it cools. Store in the freezer in the quantities you are most likely to require for use in recipes.

Hollandaise Sauce

3 egg yolks
2 Tbsp (30 ml) lemon juice
¼ level tsp (1.25 ml) salt
pinch of white pepper
7 Tbsp (100 g) unsalted butter,
   cut into 4 pieces

1

Beat the egg yolks, lemon juice, salt and pepper together in a small bowl.

2

Put the butter in a large bowl and microwave on HIGH for 1 minute or until just melted.

3

Stir the egg yolk mixture into the melted butter, then whisk thoroughly with a balloon whisk. Microwave on HIGH for 45 seconds or until the sauce is just thick enough to coat the back of a spoon, whisking every 15 seconds during cooking.

4

Remove from the oven and continue whisking for about 20 seconds to thicken the sauce further. Serve hot. If serving cold, cover the surface with plastic wrap and leave until cold. Stir before serving.

Makes 1¼ cups (300 ml).

Note The sauce can be reheated gently on LOW, whisking often. Do not reheat on HIGH.

Sauce fines herbes
Add ½ tsp (2.5 ml) chopped fresh parsley and 1 tsp (5 ml) chopped fresh tarragon.

Cucumber Sauce

½ cucumber
3 egg yolks
2 Tbsp (30 ml) lemon juice
¼ level tsp (1.25 ml) salt
pinch of white pepper
7 Tbsp (100 g) unsalted butter,
   cut into 4 pieces

1

Peel and purée the cucumber in a blender. Set aside.

2

Beat the egg yolks, lemon juice, salt and pepper together in a small bowl.

3

Put the butter in a large bowl and microwave on HIGH for 1 minute or until just melted.

4

Stir the egg yolk mixture into the melted butter, then whisk thoroughly with a balloon whisk. Microwave on HIGH for 45 seconds or until the sauce is just thick enough to coat the back of a spoon, whisking every 15 seconds during cooking.

5

Remove from the oven and continue whisking for about 20 seconds to thicken the sauce further. Stir in the puréed cucumber. Serve hot or cold with fish.

Makes about 1¼ cups (300 ml).

Sauce Raifort

3 egg yolks
2 Tbsp (30 ml) tarragon vinegar
¼ level tsp (1.25 ml) salt
pinch of white pepper
7 Tbsp (100 g) unsalted butter,
   cut into 4 pieces
3 level Tbsp (45 ml) grated
   horseradish, or prepared

1

Beat the egg yolks, vinegar, salt and pepper together in a small bowl.

2

Put the butter in a large bowl and microwave on HIGH for 1 minute or until just melted.

3

Stir the egg yolk mixture into the melted butter, then whisk thoroughly with a balloon whisk. Microwave on HIGH for 45 seconds or until the sauce is just thick enough to coat the back of a spoon, whisking every 15 seconds during cooking.

4

Remove from the oven and continue whisking for about 20 seconds to thicken the sauce further. Stir in the grated horseradish. Serve hot or cold with smoked fish or roast beef.

Makes about 1¼ cups (300 ml).

Tagliatelle with Walnut and Spinach Sauce (page 86) in a Corningware vision range saucepan.

Thick Mayonnaise Sauce

3 eggs
2 Tbsp (30 ml) lemon juice
¼ level tsp (1.25 ml) salt
pinch of white pepper
7 Tbsp (100 g) unsalted butter,
    cut into 4 pieces
5 Tbsp (75 ml) heavy cream,
    whipped
5 Tbsp (75 ml) mayonnaise

1

Beat the egg yolks, lemon juice, salt and pepper together in a small bowl.

2

Put the butter in a large bowl and microwave on HIGH for 1 minute or until just melted.

3

Stir the egg yolk mixture into the melted butter, then whisk thoroughly with a balloon whisk. Microwave on HIGH for 45 seconds or until the sauce is just thick enough to coat the back of a spoon, whisking every 15 seconds during cooking.

4

Remove from the oven and continue whisking for about 20 seconds to thicken the sauce further. Fold in the whipped cream and the mayonnaise. Cover the surface with plastic wrap and leave until cold. Serve with cold chicken.

Makes about 2 cups (450 ml).

Strawberry Cheesecake (page 103)

Butterscotch Almond Sauce

½ cup (50 g) sliced almonds
½ cup (100 g) dark brown sugar
1 cup (175 g) molasses or dark
    corn syrup
¼ cup (50 g) butter
1 cup (240 ml) evaporated milk
2 Tbsp (30 ml) lemon juice

1

Spread the almonds evenly in a pie plate and microwave on HIGH for about 5 minutes or until browned. Watch as they brown very fast in the center, so stir several times to obtain even browning. Cool.

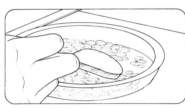

2

Combine the sugar, syrup and butter in a medium 1½-quart (1.1-liter) bowl and microwave on HIGH for 2 minutes until melted. Add the evaporated milk, beating until smooth, then beat in the lemon juice. Stir in the almonds. To serve hot, reheat on HIGH for about 2 minutes. Serve hot or cold, spooned over sponge puddings or ice cream.

Makes 2 cups (450 ml).

Note The sauce can be stored in the refrigerator for 3–4 days. Add a little extra evaporated milk if it appears too thick after storing.

Sabayon Sauce

½ cup (75 g) granulated sugar
4 egg yolks
5 Tbsp (75 ml) Madeira

1

Put the sugar in a 1-quart (0.85 liter) bowl. Beat the egg yolks and Madeira in a small cup.

2

Strain the egg yolk mixture into the sugar and microwave on HIGH for 1¼ minutes or until the sugar has dissolved. Whisk twice. Continue to cook on LOW for 1½ minutes until the sauce thickens. Using a balloon whisk, whisk every 30 seconds during cooking.

3

Remove from the microwave oven. If serving hot, use immediately with sponge fingers or over sponge pudding. To serve cold, cover the surface with plastic wrap and leave to cool. Stir before serving. Goes well with fresh fruit.

Makes ¾ cup (175 ml).

Chocolate Mocha Sauce

¼ cup (50 g) granulated sugar
4 oz (100 g) semisweet chocolate
　morsels
½ level tsp (2.5 ml) instant coffee
　powder
1 level tsp (5 ml) cornstarch
1 Tbsp (15 ml) milk
½ tsp (2.5 ml) vanilla extract

1

Mix ⅔ cup (150 ml) water and the
sugar together in a large measuring
cup and microwave on HIGH for 3
minutes or until a thin syrup is
formed. Stir every minute.

2

Stir in the chocolate and instant
coffee. Microwave on HIGH for 30
seconds then stir well.

3

Blend the cornstarch, milk and
vanilla together and stir into the
sauce. Microwave on HIGH for 3
minutes or until the mixture boils
and thickens. Stir once during
cooking and once at the end of
cooking. Cover with cling film and
leave to cool.

Makes about 1 cup (240 ml).

Marshmallow Sauce

⅔ cup (125 g) sugar
pinch of salt
8 large marshmallows
½ tsp (2.5 ml) vanilla extract
1 egg white

1

Combine the sugar, salt and ⅓ cup
(75 ml) water in a 1½-quart (1.1-
liter) ovenproof glass bowl.
Microwave on HIGH for 3 minutes
or until a thin syrup is formed and
all the sugar is dissolved. Stir every
minute during cooking.

2

Add the marshmallows and
microwave on HIGH for 45 seconds
or until the marshmallows melt.
Stir in the vanilla extract.

3

Whisk the egg white until soft
peaks form, then whisk into the
marshmallow mixture, adding
flavoring and coloring. Beat well
before serving as this sauce tends
to separate. Serve over ice cream.

Makes 2 cups (450 ml).

Fruit Marshmallow Sauce
Fold 1 lb (450 g) puréed
raspberries, strawberries or
blackberries into the sauce before
serving over ice cream.

Peppermint Sauce

⅔ cup (125 g) sugar
pinch of salt
8 large marshmallows
½ tsp (2.5 ml) vanilla extract
1 egg white
few drops of peppermint
　flavoring
few drops of green food
　coloring

1

Combine the sugar, salt and ⅔ cup
(150 ml) water in a 1½-quart (1.1-
liter) ovenproof glass lipped bowl.
Microwave on HIGH for 3 minutes
or until a thin syrup is formed and
all the sugar is dissolved. Stir every
minute during cooking.

2

Add the marshmallows and
microwave on HIGH for 45
seconds or until the marshmallows
melt. Stir in the vanilla flavoring.

3

Whisk the egg whites until soft
peaks form, then whisk into the
marshmallow mixture. Flavor with
peppermint to taste. Stir before
serving over chocolate ice cream.

Makes 2 cups (450 ml).

Note Peppermint flavorings vary
widely in strength—peppermint
extract and peppermint oil, for
instance, are far more
concentrated than peppermint
"flavoring."

Orange Sauce

2 Tbsp (25 g) unsalted butter
1 level Tbsp (15 ml) cornstarch
2 level Tbsp (30 ml) sugar
$\frac{1}{3}$ cup (75 ml) orange juice
　concentrate
1 Tbsp (15 ml) rum

1

Put the butter in a 1½-quart
(1.1-liter) ovenproof glass bowl
and microwave on HIGH for 30
seconds or until melted.

2

Add the cornstarch and sugar and
blend thoroughly. Gradually mix
in the orange juice and 1 cup
(240 ml) water and stir thoroughly.
Microwave on HIGH for 4 minutes
or until the sauce boils up and
thickens. Whisk every minute
during cooking.

3

Stir in the rum. Serve warm with
sponge puddings or gingerbread or
cover and leave to cool and serve
with ice cream, fresh strawberries
or canned pears.

Makes 1¼ cups (300 ml).

Flambé Fruit Sauce

13¼-oz (376-g) can crushed
　pineapple or other fruit in
　syrup
1 level Tbsp (15 ml) cornstarch
2 pinches of ground ginger
8 Tbsp (120 ml) apricot jam
¼ cup (50 g) butter, cut into 4
　pieces
4 Tbsp (60 ml) brandy

1

Empty the pineapple and its syrup
into a large ovenproof glass bowl.
Stir in the cornstarch, ginger, jam
and butter.

2

Microwave on HIGH for 3 minutes.
Stir and microwave on HIGH for a
further 3 minutes or until the
sauce thickens, stirring every 30
seconds during this part of the
cooking period.

3

Purée in a blender if wished. Pour
into an ovenproof glass cup and
microwave on HIGH for 2 minutes
until hot.

4

Put the brandy into a small bowl or
glass and microwave on HIGH for
5 seconds to warm. Pour over the
sauce and light with a taper. Stir
in before serving. Serve with ice
cream or hot puddings.

Makes 2 cups (450 ml).

Piquant Plum Sauce

5 Tbsp (75 ml) red wine vinegar
1 Tbsp (15 ml) Worcestershire
　sauce
3 level Tbsp (45 ml) plum jam
1 level tsp (5 ml) Dijon-style
　mustard
2 level Tbsp (30 ml) light brown
　sugar

1

Mix all the ingredients together in
a large ovenproof glass measuring
cup and microwave on HIGH for 3
minutes or until boiling rapidly.
Stir thoroughly.

2

Press the sauce through a sieve or
purée in a blender.

Makes $\frac{1}{3}$ cup (75 ml).

Note Serve with microwaved
pork chops. Serves 4.

CHAPTER NINE

Desserts

The microwave oven can be used for a whole range of desserts, from simple fruit compotes to creamy rice puddings. Use it for fast baking of egg custards and rice puddings or to prepare the sauces for a fruit crumble. Use it also to make a wonderful array of steamed English-style puddings, normally very time-consuming affairs. It is likewise useful for quick thawing of fruits from the freezer—whether they are to be cooked or eaten raw. For thawing times, see the chart at the bottom of this page.

Baking desserts in the oven

A basic pudding or crumble is ready with the help of a microwave oven in less than 10 minutes. Grease your bowl or dish and pour in the mixture. Cover the mixture with plastic wrap, making a very loose tent of the covering if the pudding will expand during cooking. Let the dish stand before turning it out, if that is the way it is served, so that the moisture in the lower part of the mixture is trapped in and slows down the cooking in that area.

Cooking fruit

Any fruit can be cooked in the microwave oven whether fresh, frozen or dried. The fruit retains its color and flavor and will cook to prefection whether you require large crunchy pieces or soft stewed purée. The speed of cooking can be quite amazing.

Piercing skinned fruits

All fruit and vegetables enclosed in a skin are likely to burst when cooked in the microwave oven because there is no external dry heat to soften the skins first. So, after coring, score round the waist of whole shiny fruits such as cooking apples to allow the steam to escape and if you pierce fruit such as cherries, it will help the fruit to keep its shape during cooking. Plums do not require piercing but they should be cooked covered as the skins will pop during cooking.

Stewing fruit

When stewing high water content fruits, such as rhubarb, no extra water is needed, provided the dish is covered completely. The full flavor of the fruit is therefore undiluted in the finished dish. Small berries such as cherries and currants will be more tender if enough water is added to just cover them. Dried fruits need no soaking before cooking in the microwave oven but enough water must be added to allow for absorption without overcooking.

Thawing and blanching fruit

Use the microwave oven to thaw frozen fruit even if you intend to eat it raw. But do this on LOW so that the pieces remain whole. You run the risk of par-cooking if you thaw on HIGH. Partially thaw and follow by a standing time at room temperature to complete the process. Use the microwave oven for blanching fruit for the freezer, too. It is particularly useful for fruit such as apple slices which discolor quickly.

Cook fruit in the microwave oven for purées, fools and crumbles and if you want to make a traditional fruit pie, cook the fruit in the microwave oven first and then combine it with the pastry, and finish in the conventional oven. When making crumble, use a deep rectangular dish because with this shape the steam escapes more easily from the boiling fruit syrup.

Thawing frozen fruit

Fruit	Time on LOW: 450 g (1 lb)
Apples, sliced	6 minutes
Apricots, halved	6 minutes plus 20 minutes standing time
Berries, soft	6 minutes
Currants, black and red	6 minutes
Peaches, whole	6 minutes plus 20 minutes standing time
Plums	8 minutes plus 10 minutes standing time
Raspberries	6 minutes
Strawberries	6 minutes
Rhubarb	4 minutes (on HIGH)

Basic Sponge Pudding

½ cup (100 g) butter or
  margarine, softened
⅔ cup (100 g) light brown sugar
2 egg, beaten
⅔ cup (100 g) self-rising flour
¼–½ tsp (1.25–2.5 ml) vanilla
  extract
1 Tbsp (15 ml) milk

For the syrup topping
2 Tbsp (30 ml) jam

1

Grease a 1-quart (0.85-liter)
ovenproof deep bowl. Beat the
butter or margarine and sugar
together until light and fluffy.

2

Add a little of the beaten egg and
1 level Tbsp (15 ml) of the flour and
beat again. Then beat in the
remaining egg.

3 .

Fold in the rest of the flour, blend
the vanilla and milk together and
gently stir into the mixture to
form a heavy batter.

4

Put the jam into the base of the
greased basin and spoon the batter
on top. Cover the basin very
loosely with plastic wrap, pressing
it close in at the sides of the bowl
but pulling it high above the center
of the pudding so that it is very
loose and wrinkly.

5

Microwave on HIGH for 3 minutes
or until the pudding is just dry on
top and shrinks away from the
sides of the basin. Leave to stand
for 5 minutes or until cooked
underneath, then remove the
plastic wrap carefully and turn the
pudding out on to a warm dish.

Serves 4.

Fruity Sponge Pudding

½ cup (100 g) butter or
  margarine, softened
⅔ cup (100 g) light brown sugar
2 eggs, beaten
⅔ cup (100 g) self-rising flour
1 Tbsp (15 ml) milk
2–3 Tbsp (30–45 ml) raisins

1

Follow Steps 1 and 2 of Basic
Sponge Pudding. Add the raisins
and fold in the remaining flour.

2

Stir the mixture together to
evenly distribute the fruit.

3

Spoon the butter into the
prepared bowl. Cover loosely with
plastic wrap as in Step 4 of the
Basic Sponge Pudding. Complete
the cooking as in Step 5.

Spicy syrup pudding
Add ground ginger and warmed
jam to the mixture before cooking.

**Basic sponge pudding with
sweet sauce**
Omit the toppings and serve with a
plain sweet sauce.

Chocolate Banana Sponge Pudding

½ cup (100 g) butter or
  margarine, softened
⅔ cup (100 g) granulated sugar
2 bananas, peeled and freshly
  mashed
⅔ cup (100 g) self-rising flour,
  sifted
2 eggs, beaten
¼–½ tsp (1.25–2.5 ml) vanilla
  extract
4 oz (100 g) semisweet
  chocolate
banana slices to decorate

1

Grease a 1½-quart (1.1-liter) deep
bowl. Beat the butter and the
sugar together until light and fluffy.
Mix in the banana and 1 level Tbsp
(15 ml) of the flour. Gradually beat
in eggs and vanilla, then fold in
remaining flour.

2

Put the mixture in the bowl and
cover loosely with plastic wrap,
pressing it close in at the sides but
pulling it high above the center of
the pudding to allow for rising.
Microwave on HIGH for 4 minutes
or until the mixture is just dry on
top. Leave for 5 minutes, then turn
out on to a serving dish.

3

Meanwhile, break up the chocolate
and put it in a basin. Microwave on
HIGH for 2½ minutes or until the
chocolate begins to melt. Stir well.
Pour the chocolate over the hot
pudding, spreading it smoothly.
Decorate with a few slices of
banana just before serving.

Serves 4–6.

Baked Egg Custard

2 cups (450 ml) milk
3 eggs, lightly beaten
$\frac{1}{4}$ cup (40 g) granulated sugar
$\frac{1}{4}$ tsp (1.25 ml) vanilla extract
pinch of ground nutmeg

1

Put the milk in a large measuring cup and microwave on HIGH for 1$\frac{1}{2}$ minutes or until it is warm to the touch.

2

Add the beaten eggs, sugar and vanilla and beat well. Strain the mixture into a 1-quart (900-ml) undecorated soufflé dish. Sprinkle over the nutmeg.

3

Three quarters cover the dish with plastic wrap. Reduce the setting and microwave on LOW for 12 minutes or until the outside of the custard is set and the center is still wobbly. Give the dish a quarter-turn three times during the cooking period.

4

Leave to stand for 10 minutes, still covered, then remove the plastic wrap and leave to cool. The custard will continue thickening during the cooling time. Chill before serving.

Serves 4.

Chocolate, Rum and Raisin Pudding

2$\frac{1}{4}$ cups (568 ml) milk
$\frac{1}{4}$ cup (40 g) semolina
$\frac{1}{3}$ cup (50 g) granulated sugar
1 Tbsp (15 g) butter or margarine
$\frac{1}{2}$ cup (60 g) raisins
2 oz (50 g) semisweet chocolate, roughly chopped, or morsels
1 Tbsp (15 ml) dark rum

1

Put the milk in a 3-quart (2.8-liter) bowl and microwave on HIGH for 5 minutes or until boiling.

2

Add the semolina, sugar and butter, stir and microwave on HIGH for 7 minutes or until the mixture thickens to the consistency of a pouring sauce. Stir twice during the first minute and twice during the remainder of the cooking time.

3

Add the raisins and microwave on HIGH for 1 minute.

4

Add the chocolate and stir until melted, then stir in the rum. Pour into individual dishes and serve hot or cold.

Serves 4.

Note The pudding thickens and the raisins soften additionally during cooling.

Bread and Butter Pudding

3 Tbsp (40 g) butter or margarine
4 thin slices wholewheat bread
$\frac{1}{4}$ cup (40 g) light brown sugar
$\frac{3}{4}$ cup (75 g) mixed raisins and currants
1$\frac{1}{4}$ cups (300 ml) milk
2 eggs
$\frac{1}{4}$ level tsp (1.25 ml) ground cinnamon
$\frac{1}{4}$ level tsp (1.25 ml) grated nutmeg

1

Butter the bread and cut each slice into quarters diagonally.

2

Place 1 Tbsp (15 g) sugar and half the fruit in the base of a lightly oiled 1-quart (0.85 liter) baking or gratin dish. Then cover with half the bread, butter side up and overlapping the pieces.

3

Cover with the remaining sugar and fruit and top with the rest of the bread (also butter side up).

4

Put the milk in a cup or bowl and microwave on HIGH for 45 seconds or until warm to the touch. Beat the eggs and spices together and stir in the milk.

5

Pour the milk mixture over the bread and microwave on LOW for 12 minutes or until the center is nearly set. Give the dish a quarter-turn three times during cooking.

6

Brown under a hot broiler (this is only possible if the baking dish is flameproof).

Serves 4.

Strawberry Cheesecake

5 Tbsp (75 g) butter
1½ cups (175 g) finely crushed
    plain tea biscuits
8 oz (225 g) cream cheese
8 oz (225 g) cottage cheese
⅔ cup (100 g) granulated sugar
2 level tsp (10 ml) grated lemon
    rind
1½ tsp (7.5 ml) lemon juice
3 eggs, beaten
⅓ cup strawberry jelly
2 cups (225 g) sliced fresh
    strawberries
whipped cream (optional)

1

Put the butter in a 9-inch (23-cm) round shallow dish and microwave on HIGH for about 45 seconds until melted. Mix in the crumbs and press the mixture thoroughly into the base and sides.

2

Microwave on HIGH for 1–1½ minutes to set the crust.

3

Beat the cheeses, sugar, lemon rind and juice and eggs thoroughly together and pour evenly into the crumb base in the dish. Microwave on HIGH for 3 minutes, giving the dish a half-turn after 1½ minutes.

4

Reduce the setting and microwave on LOW for 14 minutes or until the center is almost set. Give the dish a quarter-turn every 2 minutes during cooking.

5

Remove from the microwave oven and loosely tent with foil, leaving a gap to prevent condensation. Cool.

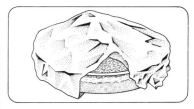

6

When the cheesecake is cool, transfer to the refrigerator and chill for at least 3 hours. If you wish to turn the cake out before decorating, freeze until hard then dip the base of the dish into warm water and unmold.

7

Meanwhile prepare the decoration. Place the jelly in a measuring cup and microwave on HIGH for 1 minute or until the water is hot. Stir thoroughly to dissolve the jelly. Leave until beginning to set.

8

Arrange the sliced strawberries on the cheesecake and pour the jelly over just before it begins to set. Refrigerate until set.

9

When the jelly is set, pipe rosettes of whipped cream around the edges, if you wish.

Serves 6–8.

Rice Pudding

½ cup (50 g) raw rice
2 Tbsp (25 g) granulated sugar
½ Tbsp (7 g) butter or
    margarine
2¼ cups (568 ml) milk
½ level tsp (2.5 ml) grated
    nutmeg

1

Mix all the ingredients thoroughly together in a 3-quart (2.8-liter) mixing bowl.

2

Microwave on HIGH for 8 minutes or until the mixture begins to boil. Stir twice during cooking.

3

Reduce the setting and microwave on LOW for 35 minutes or until the rice is soft and the pudding creamy. Stir four times during cooking. Serve hot or cold.

Serves 4.

Note Rice pudding thickens as it cools and if you prefer to eat it cold, you will find it much improved the second day. Keep in the refrigerator. A creamier rice pudding can be made using evaporated milk, combining equal quantities of milk and water.

Fruit Fondue

a selection of fresh fruit
(allowing 1 fruit per person):
apples, bananas, pears,
pineapple, oranges,
strawberries, peaches,
apricots, kiwi fruit, mangoes
lemon juice
Marshmallow sauce (page 98)
8 oz (225 g) thawed raspberries
or blackberries, puréed
green food coloring
peppermint flavoring
Sabayon sauce (page 97)
Orange sauce (page 99)
Chocolate mocha sauce
(page 98)

1

Prepare the fruit, peeling and
coring where necessary. Peel and
divide the orange into segments
but do not remove the
membranes. Leave strawberries
whole. Cut large fruit into bite-
size chunks. Toss fruit that might
discolor in lemon juice. This
includes apples, pears and bananas.

2

Arrange the fruit on a large round
dish in a decorative cartwheel
shape, mixing so that pale colors
are beside the more strident
colors. Cover with a few sheets of
paper towels to mop up any excess
moisture.

3

Into half the Marshmallow sauce
stir the puréed raspberries or
blackberries. Leave one-quarter of
the sauce plain and flavor the
remainder with 1 drop of green
coloring and 1–2 drops of
peppermint flavoring.

4

Put the 6 sauces into separate
serving bowls and arrange them in
a semi-circle round the fruit
platter. Intersperse them with
bundles of toothpicks arranged in
small glasses or serviette rings.
Have plenty of serving spoons
ready beside the sauces.

Fresh Pineapple Flambé

2 Tbsp (25 g) unsalted butter or
margarine
4 medium-thick slices fresh
pineapple, trimmed
3 Tbsp (15 g) confectioners
sugar
3 Tbsp (45 ml) kirsch

1

Put the butter in a shallow
ovenproof serving dish and
microwave on HIGH for 45 seconds
or until melted.

2

Add the pineapple slices and turn
so that they are coated on both
sides. Sift the confectioners sugar
over the buttered pineapple.

3

Microwave on HIGH for 2 minutes,
then turn the pineapple pieces
over and stir any unmixed sugar
into the butter. Microwave on
HIGH for 1 minute. Remove the
dish from the microwave oven.

4

Put the kirsch in a cup or glass and
microwave on HIGH for 5 seconds
or until warm. Pour the kirsch
evenly over the pineapple and
flambé immediately. Serve hot.

Serves 4.

Note It is safer to use a lighted
taper rather than a match to ignite
the kirsch.
    You can prepare other fruits to
flambé such as peaches or apricots
in brandy, thick apple slices in
apple brandy, pear quarters or
halves in orange-flavored liqueur,
cherries in cherry brandy.

Orange Sorbet

1¼ cups (300 ml) unsweetened
orange juice
juice of ½ lemon
½ cup (75 g) granulated sugar
1 egg white

1

Put the orange juice in a 2-cup
(0.55-liter) ovenproof glass
measuring cup and add the lemon
juice. Stir in the sugar. Microwave
on HIGH for 3 minutes or until the
sugar is dissolved, stirring from
time to time.

2

Cover the cup and put into the
freezer. Turn out the orange
mixture when firm but not frozen.
Beat thoroughly until opaque.

3

Whisk the egg white until stiff.
Fold into the half frozen orange
mixture and pour into a freezer
container. Seal the container and
return to the freezer.

4

Soften in the refrigerator for 30
minutes before serving.

Serves 8.

Dried Fruit Compote

12 oz (350 g) mixed dried fruits
   (apricots, apples, pears,
   peaches, small prunes and
   quartered figs)
$\frac{1}{2}$ cup (75 g) seedless raisins
2 Tbsp (30 ml) clear honey
2 Tbsp (30 ml) lemon juice
$2\frac{1}{2}$ cups (600 ml) water

1

Put all the fruit into a large
casserole and add water.

2

Cover with the lid and microwave
on HIGH for 10 minutes or until
almost tender, stirring once during
cooking.

3

Stir in the honey and lemon juice,
then replace the lid and leave to
stand for 30 minutes. Serve warm
or cold.

Serves 4.

Note If preferred, omit the honey
and add 2–3 Tbsp (25–50 g) brown
or white sugar to the fruit.

Stewed Dried Fruit

Put the fruit, water and sugar if used in a dish making sure that there is
sufficient water for the fruit to absorb. Cook covered, stirring during
cooking. Allow a standing time before uncovering.

	Figs whole	Figs cut up	Apricots, Peaches and Pears	Prunes
Quantity	1 lb (450 g)	1 lb (450 g)	8 oz (225 g)	1 lb (450 g)
Pre-soak	Yes—cover with water in deep dish and leave for 2 hours	No	No	No
Sugar	Add to taste after soaking	Only add if required	Add toward end of cooking time	Add half-way through cooking time
Water	No extra required	$2\frac{1}{2}$ cups (600 ml)	$2\frac{1}{2}$ cups (600 ml)	$2\frac{1}{2}$ cups (600 ml)
Microwave on HIGH	10 minutes, stir occasionally	10 minutes, stir occasionally	20 minutes, covered, stir frequently	15 minutes, three-quarters cover. Stir 3 times
Standing time	—	30 minutes	10 minutes	15 minutes

RAISINS AND CURRANTS—To plump before using in cakes put in a bowl,
barely cover with water or fruit juice, cover and microwave on HIGH for 5
minutes. Stir and leave to stand for 5 minutes.

Apple and Blackberry Crunch

12 oz (350 g) cooking apples, peeled, cored and sliced
8 oz (225 g) blackberries or blueberries
¼ cup (50 g) sugar

For the topping
2 Tbsp (25 g) butter or margarine
2 Tbsp (30 ml) honey or molasses
¼ cup (25 g) cornflakes
⅔ cup (150 ml) heavy cream

1

Put the sliced apples, the blackberries and sugar in a large ovenproof glass bowl, three-quarters cover with plastic wrap and microwave on HIGH for 5 minutes or until the fruit is soft. Stir occasionally during the cooking time.

2

Purée the fruit in a blender, then divide between 4 individual dishes or glasses and leave until cool.

3

Put the butter and honey in an ovenproof glass bowl and microwave on HIGH for 45 seconds or until melted. Stir thoroughly. Stir in the cornflakes but do not crush them.

4

Whip the cream until stiff. Cover the puréed fruit with the cream and top with the cooled cornflake topping mixture.

Serves 4.

Apple Crumble

1 cup (175 g) all-purpose flour
pinch of salt
6 Tbsp (75 g) butter or margarine
⅔ cup (100 g) granulated or light brown sugar
1½ lb (700 g) cooking apples
ground cloves

1

Sift the flour and salt into a mixing bowl and rub in the butter until the mixture resembles fine breadcrumbs. Stir in ¼ cup (40 g) of the sugar.

2

Peel, core, quarter and thinly slice the apples and spread evenly in a deep dish. Add ⅓ cup (50 g) sugar and ground cloves to taste.

3

Cover and microwave on HIGH for 5 minutes or until the apples begin to soften.

4

Top with the crumble mixture, pressed well down, and sprinkle with the remaining sugar and a pinch of ground cloves. Without covering, microwave on HIGH for 10–12 minutes or until just set. Give the dish a quarter-turn every 3 minutes during cooking. Do not overcook. Allow several minutes longer cooking time if the crumble topping has been taken direct from the freezer and the fruit is frozen or cold.

Serves 4.

Note The apple may bubble up while the crumble is cooking but will settle again, leaving the crumble intact when cooking is finished.

Summer Sponge Pudding

8 oz (225 g) fresh or frozen cherries, stoned
12 oz (350 g) fresh or frozen blackberries
4 oz (125 g) fresh or frozen raspberries
⅓ cup (65 g) granulated sugar
whipped cream to serve

For the sponge cake lining
3 eggs
½ cup (75 g) granulated sugar
few drops of vanilla extract
1 Tbsp (15 ml) vegetable oil
½ cup (75 g) all-purpose flour

1

Grease a 1-quart (0.85-liter) deep bowl. Mix the cherries, blackberries, raspberries and sugar together in an ovenproof glass bowl. Three-quarters cover with plastic wrap and microwave on HIGH for 5 minutes or until the fruit juices run (the fruit should not be cooked). Set aside while preparing the sponge mixture.

2

Cut two 12-inch (30.5-cm) circles from waxed paper and grease on one side. Take out the oven shelf unless it is fixed and put the paper on it, or put the waxed paper on a piece of cardboard or suitable tray that will fit into the oven cavity comfortably.

3

Whisk the eggs, sugar and vanilla together until pale and mousse-like; a fork drawn through the mixture should form a trail. Sprinkle the oil over the surface and fold in lightly.

4

Sift half the flour over the mixture and fold in, then sift the remaining flour over the mixture and fold in lightly and rapidly.

5

Pour the sponge mixture on to 1 piece of prepared paper to reach within 2 inches (5 cm) of the edge. Lift the shelf, turntable or cardboard with the sponge-topped waxed paper still in position and put it into the microwave oven. If cardboard has been used slip this out carefully.

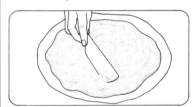

6

Microwave on HIGH for 3 minutes, then cover the sponge with the other paper circle, greased side against the sponge, and microwave on HIGH for 2 minutes or until the top is dry (the outside edges may still be slightly moist but do not cook further).

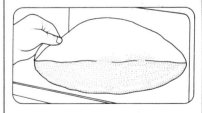

7

Remove the shelf or turntable from the oven and take off the paper cover. Slide a long palette knife between the cake mixture and the paper to make sure that it will come away easily. Cut out a wedge (about $\frac{1}{3}-\frac{1}{4}$ of the cake), then using your hands, lift the cake disc carefully and fit into the prepared bowl to line it. Push the edges to ease the cake into the base.

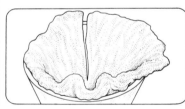

8

Reserve $\frac{2}{3}$ cup (150 ml) of the fruit juices and a little of the fruit, then pour the remainder of the fruit into the basin. Cover the middle with the cut-out cake wedge and fold the edges of the cake lining over to completely enclose the fruit. Using a cup, pour the reserved fruit juice over the top and around the sides of the pudding so that it is completely soaked.

9

Cover the basin loosely with plastic wrap and press a saucer on the top. Place a heavy weight on top of the saucer, then put the basin in a cool place or refrigerate at least 12 hours or overnight.

10

Loosen the pudding with a knife and turn out on to a serving dish. Pour the reserved juices and fruit over the pudding, making sure that any unsoaked parts are covered, and serve with whipped cream.

Serves 4–6.

Note To speed up the whisking of the eggs and sugar, take the chill off the eggs by putting them in the microwave oven for 5 seconds only, set on HIGH; take the chill off the sugar by placing the mixing bowl in the microwave oven on HIGH for 2 minutes. If the mixture is still too slow to thicken, microwave the foamy egg and sugar mixture on DEFROST for 20 seconds before continuing to whisk. This is the equivalent of whisking over hot water in the conventional way.

Traditional Summer Pudding can be made using the fruits as given in the Summer Sponge Pudding, increasing the sugar to $\frac{1}{2}$ cup (100 g). Take 4–6 bread slices and cut off the crusts. Trim the bread to line the base and sides of the baking dish. Fill with most of the fruit and the juice. Cover the fruit with bread.

Cover loosely with plastic wrap, put a saucer and weights on top and refrigerate for at least 12 hours. Turn out and serve with the reserved fruit and juices and cream.

CHAPTER TEN

Baking

There are many advantages in using the microwave oven for baking. There is no waste of valuable fuel, such as occurs when a large conventional oven has to be heated for just one cake and neither is preheating required. There are no baked-on tins to scour and the cakes are ready in no time at all.

But microwave baking has its limitations. Because of the nature of microwaves it is only possible to either bake crisp throughout or soft throughout; you cannot get a crisp crust and a soft center. The moist heat obtained by microwaves keeps the crust soft and, incidentally, gives cakes a higher rise. Make sure that your cake containers are large enough to allow for this extra rising and only half-fill them. Any mixture that rises more than $\frac{1}{2}$ inch (1 cm) above the container will spill over.

The shape of the container is important in baking. The use of a ring mold ensures an even overall texture. Round dishes should not be more than 9 inches (23 cm) in diameter and choose square dishes with rounded corners to prevent overcooking in the angles.

Shallow containers cook faster than deep and two shallow cakes cooked separately will take about the same time as one deep cake.

Cakes baked in loaf-shaped dishes tend to cook first at the ends before the center is ready. When the ends are cooked, cover them with smooth pieces of foil and continue microwaving until the middle has caught up. Bake small cakes in double paper cases or in specialist bun tins.

Since browning doesn't occur in the microwave oven, use dark-colored ingredients such as dark brown sugar, malt extract, molasses or dark-colored spices to darken baked mixtures. Chocolate cakes, ginger cakes and similar items require no embellishment but lighter cake mixtures must be iced or decorated in some way. When time is short freshly whipped cream is an excellent disguise.

Preparation of Containers

Generally speaking plastic re-usable containers designed for microwave cooking need no greasing unless the mixture contains only a small amount of fat. Ovenproof glass dishes do need greasing and it is always a good idea to line the base of a cake dish with a circle of waxed paper in addition to greasing it all over to allow the rising cake to climb easily up the sides.

Cake containers may also be loosely lined with plastic wrap unless hot syrups or sugar mixtures are being baked in the base; this gives a cake a very smooth, shiny appearance. If a cake is being iced this is of no importance but if you find the shiny finish ugly, pare away the outer layer with a knife.

The outer layer of a cake is usually very soft on removal from the microwave oven. Do not overcook cakes, puddings or other baked items or they will harden very quickly. If they have been overcooked there is no remedy except to break them up and use them in puddings or similar dishes.

Turn out the cake immediately after the standing time to prevent it from sticking to the container. Cakes should be wrapped in plastic wrap as soon as they are cool and similarly wrap the remainder if only a few pieces have been cut.

Cookies

Although cookies can be cooked in the microwave oven the traditional crisp type do not turn out well, so it seems more sensible to use your conventional oven for these. However, when a mixture is baked in one piece and sub-sequently cut into bars, such as brownies or bar cookies, the microwave oven is efficient. This type of cookie usually has a high sugar content and will burn easily so do not overcook; burning begins in the center and you may not see it until it is too late.

Pastry

Pastry tends to be tough and dry if cooked in the microwave oven. It is much better to cook pie shells conventionally, then fill and cook the filling by microwave. For top crust pies, cook the filling by microwave first, then cover with pastry and finish cooking in the conventional oven.

Bread

Bread is not good cooked by microwave, but the microwave oven is useful for refreshing stale loaves. Likewise it does wonders for a plain cake that is past its best.

Frangipane Tart

For the pie crust
¼ cup (50 g) butter or
   margarine
1 cup (100 g) finely crushed
   sweet biscuits, such as rich
   tea

For the filling
2–3 Tbsp (30–45 ml) raspberry
   jam
¼ cup (50 g) butter or
   margarine, softened
¼ cup (50 g) granulated sugar
grated rind of 1 lemon
½ cup (50 g) fresh breadcrumbs
½ cup (50 g) ground almonds
2 eggs, beaten
½ tsp (2.5 ml) almond extract

For the topping
about ¾ cup (100 g)
   confectioners sugar, sifted
red food coloring

1

Put the butter in a 7-inch (18-cm) round cake dish (measuring diameter across the top); the depth of the baked tart is about 1¼ inches (3 cm). Microwave on HIGH for 45 seconds or until the butter is melted.

2

Mix in the biscuit crumbs thoroughly, using a fork, and press into the base and sides of the cake dish. Microwave on HIGH for 1 minute to set the mixture.

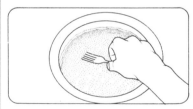

3

After a few minutes cover the base of the tart shell with a layer of raspberry jam (do not drag the jam across the surface or it will break up the shell). If necessary warm the jam for 5–10 seconds in a bowl in the microwave oven.

4

To make the filling, beat the butter and sugar together until the mixture is light and fluffy.

5

Stir in the lemon rind, fresh breadcrumbs and ground almonds, then beat in the eggs and almond flavoring.

6

Spread the filling evenly over the jam and microwave on HIGH for 2 minutes giving the dish a quarter-turn three times during cooking.

7

Reduce the setting and microwave on LOW for 5 minutes or until the center of the cake is set. Give the dish a quarter-turn three times during cooking.

8

Leave the tart in the cake dish until cool but not cold and turn out carefully on to a large plate. Immediately reverse on to a similar sized plate (do not use a wire rack). If any of the crumb crust crumbles away, it can be easily pushed back using a warm table knife.

9

Mix the confectioners sugar with 2–3 tsp (10–15 ml) water to form a thick pouring consistency. Pour evenly over the tart.

10

Dip a skewer in the red food coloring and, just before the icing sets, draw the skewer in straight lines about 1 inch (2.5 cm) apart across the surface.

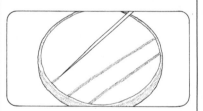

11

Leave for a few minutes for the coloring to set, then draw the cleaned skewer through the icing at right angles and at the same intervals as before but the lines should be drawn in alternate directions so that a feathering effect is achieved (for the best results hold the skewer at as flat an angle as possible). Leave until the icing has set firmly before serving. Store in an airtight container, if you wish.

Serves 8.

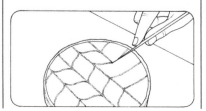

Rum and cherry truffles

10 glacé cherries
2 Tbsp (30 ml) rum
3 oz (75 g) semisweet chocolate
¼ cup (50 g) granulated sugar
¼ cup (50 g) butter or
   margarine
1 egg, lightly beaten
½ tsp (2.5 ml) vanilla extract

½ cup (65 g) all-purpose flour
½ level tsp (2.5 ml) baking
   powder
¼ cup (25 g) ground almonds
2–3 level Tbsp (30–45 ml)
   apricot jam
1 cup (100 g) chocolate
   sprinkles

1

Put the cherries and rum in a small bowl or glass and leave to soak while making the cake mixture.

2

Put the chocolate and sugar in a mixing bowl and, if using chocolate chips, stir before cooking. Microwave on HIGH for 2 minutes or until the chocolate begins to melt. Stir once during cooking. If necessary microwave on HIGH for a few more seconds until the chocolate is fully melted.

3

Add the butter and beat until it melts and blends with the melted chocolate.

4

Add the egg, vanilla flavoring, flour, baking powder and almonds and mix thoroughly. Microwave on HIGH for 1 minute, then stir to mix the half-cooked batter. Microwave on HIGH for 2½ minutes or until the mixture is dry on top.

5

Strain the rum from the cherries over the mixture and add the jam. Beat thoroughly while hot.

6

Leave to cool slightly, then divide the mixture into 10 and form 1 at a time into balls, tucking a cherry into the center of each. *Do not overwork the mixture.* As each ball is shaped toss in a very small bowl quarter-filled with chocolate vermicelli, swirling the bowl to produce even-shaped cakes. Remove carefully with a spoon, place on a dish or plate and refrigerate.

Makes 10.

Variations Use small pieces of pineapple for stuffing and flavor the mixture with kirsch, or small pieces of partly cooked dried apricots and orange-flavored liqueur. The truffles may also be made without stuffing, putting chopped raisins into the mixture after it is cooked.

Marble Ring Cake

¾ cup (175 g) light brown sugar
¾ cup (175 g) butter or
   margarine, softened
1¼ cups (175 g) all-purpose flour
1 level tsp (5 ml) baking
   powder
3 eggs, beaten
2 level Tbsp (30 ml) cocoa
   powder, sifted
1 level tsp (5 ml) grated lemon
   rind

1

Beat the sugar and butter together until the mixture is light and fluffy. Sift together the flour and baking powder. Mix 1 level Tbsp (15 ml) of the sifted flour into the butter mixture, then add the eggs gradually, beating all the time. Add remaining flour and fold in quickly.

2

Transfer half the mixture to another bowl and mix the cocoa into this. Stir in the grated lemon rind.

3

Spoon half the plain mixture into a 1-quart (1-liter) plastic ring mold, then cover with half the chocolate mixture. Repeat, finishing with chocolate mixture.

4

Without covering, microwave on HIGH for 4 minutes or until the cake is just dry on top. Give the dish a quarter-turn four times during cooking. Leave for 3–4 minutes.

Serves 8.

Note Wrap in plastic wrap as soon as it is cool. Ring molds other than the soft white plastic specialist microware should be well greased before filling.

Lemon Ginger Cake

½ cup (100 g) butter or margarine, softened
½ cup (100 g) dark brown sugar
2 eggs, beaten
2 Tbsp (30 ml) molasses
1½ cups (225 g) self-rising flour
2 level tsp (10 ml) ground ginger
½ level tsp (2.5 ml) baking soda

For the topping
3½ cups (350 g) confectioners sugar, sifted
2 Tbsp (30 ml) lemon juice
½ oz (15 g) butter or margarine, softened
pared rind of 1 lemon, cut into thin strips

1

Grease and line the bottom of an 8-inch (20.5-cm) round cake dish.

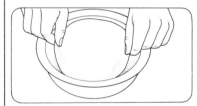

2

Beat the butter and sugar until light and creamy. Beat in eggs and molasses. Sift together the flour, ginger and baking soda, and add to the creamed mixture.

3

Spread the cake batter into the prepared dish and microwave on HIGH for 4 minutes or until the cake is only just dry on top. Give the dish a quarter-turn three times during cooking and reposition on the turntable. Leave for 5 minutes before turning out. Cool on a wire rack over a dish or plate. Decorate when cool.

4

To make the topping blend the confectioners sugar with the lemon juice and about 2 Tbsp (30 ml) water to form a thick coating icing. Add the butter and microwave on HIGH for 30 seconds or until the butter is melted, stirring occasionally during cooking.

5

Put the lemon rind strips into a glass measuring cup, just cover with water and microwave on HIGH for 4 minutes or until the water boils. Drain. Cover the lemon strips with fresh cold water and microwave on HIGH for 3 minutes or until the water reboils, then drain again. Cool.

6

Pour the icing over the cake, allowing it to dribble down the sides, and sprinkle the top of the cake with the lemon strips.

Serves 8–10.

Note This plain cake improves if kept for up to 3 days before cutting. Store it well wrapped.

Cinnamon Crumble Coffeecake

2 Tbsp (25 g) butter or margarine
⅓ cup (50 g) all-purpose flour
2 level tsp (10 ml) light brown sugar
2½ level tsp (12.5 ml) ground cinnamon
1 cup (125 g) all-purpose flour
¼ teaspoon salt
1 level tsp (5 ml) baking powder
¾ cup (125 g) light brown sugar
½ cup (125 g) butter, softened
2 eggs, lightly beaten
1 Tbsp (15 ml) orange liqueur

1

Grease and line the bottom of a 7-inch (18-cm) ovenproof glass dish or (measuring diameter across top) a 7-inch (18-cm) round cake dish.

2

Rub the butter into the flour. Mix in the sugar and the cinnamon. To make the cake, sift together the flour, salt and baking powder. Beat the sugar and butter together until light and fluffy.

3

Add the eggs to the mixture with the flour, salt and baking powder and orange liqueur. Beat thoroughly for 30 seconds.

4

Pour the mixture into the prepared dish. Microwave on HIGH for 3 minutes or until the cake is almost but not quite set. Give the dish a quarter-turn three times during cooking.

5

Sprinkle the crumble topping evenly over the cake and microwave on HIGH for 2 minutes or until the topping is cooked. Leave for 4 minutes, then turn out on to a wire rack and quickly reverse on to a second wire rack.

Serves 8.

Oat Bars

5 Tbsp (75 g) butter or
  margarine
½ cup (75 g) light brown sugar
2 Tbsp (30 ml) honey or
  molasses
1 cup (150 g) rolled oats
1 cup (125 g) self-rising flour

1

Put the butter and sugar in a 1½-
quart (1.1-liter) bowl and
microwave on HIGH for 1 minute
until melted. Stir in the honey,
oats, and flour, and mix until well
blended.

2

Spread the mixture in an 8-inch
(20-cm) baking dish and level the
surface.

3

Microwave on MEDIUM for 7
minutes, quarter-turning the dish
three times during the cooking
time. Mark into bars before the
mixture cools. When cold cover
tightly with plastic wrap.

Makes 14 bars.

Note The oat bars will soften on
storage and therefore are best
eaten fresh.

Brownies

5 Tbsp (75 g) butter or
  margarine
6 level Tbsp (90 ml) cocoa
  powder
1 cup (225 g) granulated sugar
2 eggs, beaten
2 Tbsp (30 ml) milk
½ level tsp (2.5 ml) vanilla
  extract
¾ cup (100 g) self-rising flour
½ cup (50 g) chopped walnuts

1

Put the butter and cocoa powder
in a 1½-quart (1.1-liter) bowl and
microwave on HIGH for 1½
minutes or until melted. Mix until
well blended.

2

Stir in the sugar, then add the eggs,
milk, vanilla flavoring, flour and
walnuts and beat well.

3

Pour into an 8-inch (20-cm) square
baking dish. Microwave on HIGH
for 4 minutes, quarter-turning
three times during cooking. Cool.
Cover with plastic wrap if the
brownies are to be stored.

Makes 16 squares.

Chocolate
Cookie Cake

½ cup (100 g) butter or
  margarine
2 Tbsp (30 ml) molasses or
  syrup
2 Tbsp (25 g) granulated sugar
4 oz (100 g) semisweet
  chocolate
1½ cups (175 g) roughly broken
  plain cookies or vanilla
  wafers
¼ cup (25 g) raisins
¼ cup (25 g) flaked almonds
½ cup (50 g) glacé cherries

1

Put the butter, molasses, sugar
and chocolate into a 1½-quart (1.1-
liter) ovenproof glass bowl and
microwave on HIGH for 2 minutes
or until the fat and chocolate have
melted. Stir well.

2

Add the rest of the ingredients and
mix well to coat them with the
chocolate mixture.

3

Place a 7-inch (18-cm) plain flan
ring on a flat serving plate and
spoon in the cookie mixture. Press
down evenly and chill in the
refrigerator for about 8 hours or
overnight. Remove the flan ring.

Serves 8.

Note This cake is so rich it is
almost like candy.

Malt Soda Bread

½ tsp (2.5 ml) malt extract,
   to glaze
⅔ cup (100 g) all-purpose flour
1 cup (125 g) wholewheat flour
½ level tsp (2.5 ml) salt
½ level tsp (2.5 ml) baking soda
1 Tbsp (15 g) butter or
   margarine, softened
2 Tbsp (30 ml) malt extract
1 cup (240 ml) buttermilk
flour for shaping

1

First prepare the glaze. Put the
½ tsp (2.5 ml) malt extract in a small
bowl and add ½ tsp (2.5 ml) water.
Microwave on HIGH for 20
seconds and stir well.

2

Mix the flours, salt and baking
soda thoroughly together in an
ovenproof glass mixing bowl and
microwave on HIGH for 20
seconds to warm slightly.

3

Add the butter, remaining malt
extract and buttermilk and mix to
a soft, sticky dough.

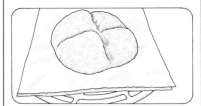

4

Shape on a lightly floured work
surface to a 6-inch (15-cm)
round and, using a long sharp knife,
make a deep cross on the top.

5

Place a sheet of paper towel on a
microwave roasting rack and
gently put the dough on top.
Microwave the bread on HIGH for
4 minutes.

6

Brush the top of the bread with
the glaze, then microwave on
HIGH for 2 minutes or until risen
and dry on top. Test with a
wooden toothpick or skewer,
which should come out clean.

7

Remove the rack from the
microwave oven, then lift the
bread and carefully peel away the
paper towel (it will be hot but
will stick if not removed at once).
Leave the bread on the rack to
cool, then serve fresh, with butter.

Makes 1 loaf.

Note Malt extract is available in
specialty food shops or health
food stores.

Black Forest Cherry Cake

½ cup (125 ml) corn syrup
½ cup (75 g) dark brown sugar
5 Tbsp (75 g) butter or
   margarine
¾ cup (100 g) self-rising flour
¼ cup (40 g) cocoa powder,
   sifted
1 egg, beaten
4 Tbsp (60 ml) milk
14-oz (425-g) can pitted black
   cherries
1¼ cups (300 ml) heavy cream,
   whipped
½ oz (15 g) semisweet chocolate,
   grated

1

Grease and base line a 7-inch (18-
cm) ovenproof glass dish or a
round cake dish.

2

Place the corn syrup, brown
sugar and butter in a 3-quart (2.8-
liter) ovenproof glass bowl and
microwave on HIGH for 2 minutes
or until melted. Stir well.

3

Add the flour and cocoa and beat
well. Beat in the egg and milk. Pour
into the prepared dish and
microwave on HIGH for 5 minutes.
Turn three times during cooking.

4

Leave to stand for 5 minutes before
turning out on to a wire rack.
When cold, cut in half horizontally
and place the base of the cake on
a serving plate. Drain the black
cherries and spoon a little of the
cherry juice over the base.

5

Spoon half the whipped cream
over the base and scatter the
cherries over the cream. Top with
the other cake layer. Pipe rosettes
of cream around the edge of the
cake and decorate with grated
chocolate.

Serves 6–8.

CHAPTER ELEVEN

Candies

Making chocolates, sweets and candies is more of a leisure pursuit than a necessity, but commercial sweets are very expensive and the high prices result more from labor costs than the price of the ingredients. Home-made candy is relatively cheap, and purer because fewer chemical ingredients are used. Many people are put off candy-making by the thought of sticky pans, burnt-on caramel and the disappointment of failure. The microwave oven will give you more successful results than a stove top because there is no direct contact between the sugary ingredients and the heat source.

Burning can still occur, but this does not happen unless the sugary ingredients are over-cooked; little can go wrong in the initial stages. Do not leave the kitchen while candies are cooking in the microwave oven. Because sugar syrups reach a very high temperature you must take the same precautions as you would when cooking conventionally. Make sure you have a good pair of non-slip oven gloves, a dry heatproof surface, wooden spoons with long handles and large cooking containers that can resist the very high temperatures. A 3-quart (2.8-liter) ovenproof glass bowl is indispensable and large glass measuring cups or lipped measuring bowls should be included in your list of equipment.

Start with the easiest process, which is melting chocolate. You will find that you are able to dip all kinds of fruit and fillings into the chocolate to produce a variety of instant sweets. After very little practice you will be able to determine when the chocolate is sufficiently softened to melt with just a stir or two. Semi-sweet chocolate melts more easily than milk chocolate and becomes thinner.

One final tip—save all your old chocolate boxes and chocolate papers. These will come in useful when making boxes of assorted candies and chocolates for giving as presents.

Melting chocolate
Break up the chocolate unless using chocolate chips and put into a bowl. Use a cup if the chocolate is to be poured, such as over a cake. If chocolate is being melted for dipping centers, choose a narrow diameter bowl so that the melted chocolate will be sufficiently deep to minimize the need for turning.

Microwave only until the chocolate is soft and glossy on top, then stir until melted. If by accident you overheat the chocolate and it becomes set and grainy, quickly beat in $\frac{1}{2}$ tsp (2.5 ml) solid white vegetable fat. Butter is not suitable for this purpose. The melting times vary according to the type of material and shape of container used, so it is adivsable to check every 1 minute during melting. Take care not to overcook or the melted chocolate may scorch.

Orange Rind Snakes

2 medium oranges
4 oz (100 g) semisweet
  chocolate

1

Put the oranges on a wooden board or work surface. Using a sharp knife and following the contour of the orange, pare away the rind and only a thin layer of the pith. Cut the rind into strips no more than $\frac{1}{4}$-inch (0.5 cm) wide and about $2\frac{1}{2}$ inches (6.5 cm) long.

2

Put the orange strips into a large glass measuring cup and just cover with cold water. Microwave on HIGH for 3 minutes or until boiling, then drain.

3

Cover with fresh cold water and microwave on HIGH for $2\frac{1}{2}$ minutes or until boiling once more. Drain thoroughly. Spread the orange strips out on paper towels to absorb any remaining moisture.

4

Break up the chocolate and put into a small bowl. Microwave on LOW for 4 minutes or until the chocolate is shiny and just begins to lose its shape. Stir until melted, microwaving for a little longer if necessary. Do not overcook or the chocolate will burn.

5

Dip the orange strips into the melted chocolate one at a time and spread out on non-stick paper. Leave until cold.

Makes about 8 oz (225 g).

Note The orange rind snakes store well in the refrigerator for a few days. This is a good way of using up the peel when you want oranges for another recipe or to eat fresh.

Marzipan Chocolate

5 oz (150 g) block marzipan, cut
  into 12 pieces approximately
  $1 \times \frac{1}{2} \times \frac{3}{4}$ inch (2.5 $\times$1 $\times$2 cm)
4 oz (100 g) semisweet
  chocolate, melted
6 whole almonds, lightly
  roasted and split in half
  lengthwise (see note)

1

Using a fork or skewer, dip the pieces of marzipan individually into the chocolate, scooping the melted chocolate over the marzipan with a table knife.

2

Lift carefully out of the bowl and place on a sheet of non-stick paper. Immediately top the chocolate with half an almond, browned side up.

3

Dip all the remaining marzipan pieces, topping with the almonds. Leave to cool. Trim off any jagged pieces of chocolate with a sharp knife (these can be remelted if more chocolate is required).

Makes 12 pieces.

Note Should the chocolate begin to set before all the marzipan pieces are dipped, replace the bowl in the microwave oven for a few seconds only, set on HIGH. $\frac{1}{4}$ cup (25 g) almonds spaced out on a plate on the microwave oven shelf will take 1 minute on HIGH to lightly roast. Stir twice during cooking.

Handmade Chocolate Truffles

3 Tbsp (45 ml) heavy cream
1½ tsp (7.5 ml) rum
2 egg yolks
two 5-oz (150-g) bars
    semisweet chocolate

1

Put the cream in a small bowl and microwave on HIGH for about 20 seconds or until boiling. Leave to cool slightly, then stir in the rum and egg yolks.

2

Put half the chocolate in a larger bowl and microwave on HIGH for 3 minutes or until melted (the chocolate is ready as soon as it becomes shiny and some of the pieces lose their shape).

3

Stir in the egg and cream mixture and beat thoroughly. Microwave on HIGH for 30 seconds, then beat again. If the mixture is not obviously thickened, microwave for a further 30 seconds, then beat again vigorously.

4

Put the bowl in the refrigerator and leave until the mixture is firm enough to mold. Beat the mixture once during cooling.

5

When the mixture is ready, using your hands, roll into small even-sized balls.

6

To coat, break up the remaining chocolate and put into a small bowl. Microwave on LOW for 4 minutes or until the chocolate begins to lose its shape, then stir until melted.

7

Drop the truffles one at a time into the melted chocolate and turn so that they are completely coated. Lift out with the curved part of a fork and put, spaced out, on a dish lined with non-stick paper. Refrigerate until the chocolate coating is set.

Makes 24 truffles, 6 oz (175 g).

Peanut Brittle

1 cup (175 g) granulated sugar
5 Tbsp (75 ml) glucose or corn
    syrup
2 Tbsp (25 g) butter or
    margarine
1¼ cups (150 g) salted peanuts
1 level tsp (5 ml) baking soda
¼ tsp (1.25 ml) vanilla extract

1

Place a sheet of waxed or non-stick paper on a heatproof surface. Oil a palette knife.

2

Place the sugar, glucose syrup and 2 Tbsp (30 ml) water in a large ovenproof glass bowl. Microwave on HIGH for 2 minutes until dissolved. Using a wooden spoon, stir in the butter. Microwave on HIGH for 1 minute until melted.

3

Stir in the peanuts and microwave on HIGH for 6 minutes until light brown. Do not stir while the peanuts are cooking.

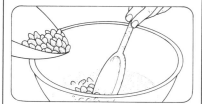

4

Meanwhile mix the bicarbonate of soda, vanilla flavoring and 1 tsp (5 ml) cold water together. As soon as the peanut mixture is ready, pour in the soda mixture and beat thoroughly with a wooden spoon for 2 minutes until the mixture "honeycombs" throughout. If the mixture is not stirred sufficiently the peanut brittle will turn tacky, not brittle.

Turkish Delight

2 Tbsp (25 g) cornstarch
¾ cup (175 g) granulated sugar
few drops of red or green
  edible food coloring
1½–2 tsp (7.5–10 ml) rose water
  or a few drops of crème de
  menthe flavoring
extra cornstarch for the mold

For coating
2 level Tbsp (30 ml) cornstarch
2 level Tbsp (30 ml)
  confectioners sugar

5

Smooth the mixture over the paper with the palette knife to ¼ inch (0.5 cm) thickness. Leave for 3 minutes as the brittle is too hot to handle.

6

Turn the mixture over on the paper while it is still pliable and leave until cool enough to touch. Pulling from the edges, stretch the brittle until the peanuts stand out of the mixture and it measures about 11 × 8 inches (28 × 20.5 cm). Pull the brittle in stages.

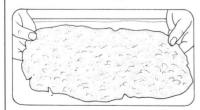

7

Leave until cold then break up into pieces and store in an airtight tin. It will keep for 1–2 weeks.

Makes 10 oz (275 g).

1

Blend the cornstarch with ⅓ cup (75 ml) water in a small bowl and set aside.

2

Combine the sugar with 1 cup (225 ml) water in a large ovenproof glass bowl and microwave on HIGH for 3 minutes. Then stir until the sugar has dissolved.

3

Add the cornstarch mixture to the sugar syrup and microwave on HIGH for 6 minutes, stirring every minute. Add either red coloring and rose flavoring, or green coloring and crème de menthe flavoring. Microwave on HIGH for 3 minutes or until the mixture is the consistency of thick jelly and will not drop easily from a spoon. Stir every minute during cooking.

4

While the Turkish delight is cooking, rub a 7½ × 3½-inch (19 × 8-cm) container (see note) lightly with oil, put in a generous quantity of cornstarch making sure that it coats not only the base but also the sides. Spoon the thick mixture as evenly as possible into the container and leave until cool.

5

Sift together the cornstarch and confectioners sugar on to a sheet of non-stick paper. Turn the set Turkish delight on to it.

6

Cut the Turkish delight into approximately 21 squares and generously coat the cut surfaces with the cornstarch and confectioners sugar mixture. Leave until cold then toss in the cornstarch mixture again. Leave uncovered for several hours until the jellies are crusty outside. Store in a box with the remainder of the cornstarch and confectioners sugar (this is to make sure that the Turkish delight keeps dry).

Makes 21 pieces.

Note Make sure that the Turkish delight mixture is fully cooked and really thick. If it is too soft when poured into the mold, it will not harden sufficiently to make it manageable. The Turkish delight dries out and becomes much firmer after about 12 hours. A foil dish is an ideal container for setting. Cut down the sides of the dish with scissors and flatten before turning out the Turkish delight.

Pineapple Chocolates

2 fresh pineapple slices
4 oz (100 g) semisweet
chocolate, melted
silver sugar balls

1

Remove the center core from fresh pineapple slices and cut the rings into bite-sized wedges. Pat very thoroughly with paper towels to remove excess moisture.

2

Using a fork or skewer dip the pineapple pieces one at a time in the melted chocolate, scooping the chocolate over with a table knife to make sure the pineapple is completely covered.

3

Put the chocolates, spaced out, on a sheet of non-stick paper and place a silver ball on each before the chocolate has set.

4

Trim the chocolates with a sharp knife when the chocolate is firm, so that they look neat. Store in the refrigerator.

Makes about 20.

Creamy Vanilla Fudge

2 Tbsp (25 g) butter
1¼ cups (225 g) granulated sugar
5 Tbsp (75 ml) sweetened
condensed milk
½ tsp (2.5 ml) vanilla extract

1

Lightly oil a small rectangular foil dish or suitable mold.

2

Put the butter into a 3-quart (2.8-liter) ovenproof glass bowl and microwave on HIGH for 30 seconds or until the butter is only just melted.

3

Stir in the sugar, milk, 4 Tbsp (60 ml) water and the vanilla flavoring and continue stirring for 1 minute until the sugar is almost dissolved. Microwave on HIGH for 2 minutes then, using oven gloves, give the bowl a gentle shake.

4

Microwave on HIGH for 6 minutes or until a spoonful of the mixture forms a soft ball when dropped into cold water.

5

Carefully remove the bowl from the microwave oven and beat constantly until the mixture is thick and creamy and tiny crystals form (do not continue beating after this or the fudge will become candy-like and granular).

6

Pour the fudge immediately into the prepared dish. Allow to cool; refrigerate overnight until cold, then turn out and cut into squares. These creamy fudges improve if stored, uncovered, in the refrigerator for 24 hours.

Makes about 12 oz (350 g), or 25.

Note For a variation make marshmallow fudge. When the mixture is removed from the microwave oven, quickly add ½ cup (50 g) chopped marshmallows, then beat until cool and continue as before. For fruit fudge, add ½ cup (50 g) chopped seeded raisins, chopped glacé cherries or dates. For nut fudge, add ½ cup (50 g) any chopped nuts. For ginger fudge, add ¼ cup (25 g) finely chopped preserved ginger.

Summer Sponge Pudding
(page 106–107)

Coconut Ice

1¼ cups (225 g) granulated sugar
pinch of cream of tartar
2 Tbsp (30 ml) sweetened
    condensed milk
¾ cup (75 g) shredded coconut
2 drops of red food coloring
2 drops of rose water

1

Have ready a small rectangular dish
or suitable mold. Put the sugar,
cream of tartar, 3 Tbsp (45 ml)
water and the condensed milk into
a large ovenproof glass bowl (it
boils up considerably). Stir well;
microwave on HIGH for 1 minute.

2

Shake the bowl gently to help the
sugar dissolve but do not stir.
Microwave on HIGH for 2 minutes
or until a spoonful of the syrup
forms a soft ball when dropped
into cold water. Test at frequent
intervals after the first 2 minutes if
the syrup needs further cooking.

3

Using oven gloves, remove the
bowl from the microwave oven
and stir in the coconut. Beat
thoroughly until the mixture
thickens, then pour half of the
mixture into the dish or mold.

4

Beat the coloring and flavoring
into the remaining mixture and
spread on top, smoothing with a
palette knife. Leave until set, then
cut into bars.

Makes 12 oz (350 g), about 8–16 bars.

**Orange Marmalade (page 122),
Blackberry Jam (page 121),
Lemon Curd (page 123) and
Strawberry Jam (page 122).**

Chocolate Peppermint Creams

2¾ cups (225 g) confectioners
    sugar, sifted
1 egg white
peppermint flavoring
green food coloring
8 oz (225 g) semisweet
    chocolate

1

Put the confectioners sugar in a
large bowl and mix in only
sufficient of the egg white to form
a stiff paste.

2

Add a few drops of peppermint
flavoring and the coloring (take
care not to add too much
flavoring or coloring as this could
ruin the peppermint creams).

3

Knead the paste in the bowl with
the fingers until it becomes
sufficiently manageable to roll,
firm but pliable.

4

Roll out to ¼ inch (0.5 cm) thick
between 2 sheets of non-stick
paper (use the rolling pin on the
paper and not directly on to the
sugar mixture).

5

Remove the top sheet of paper and
cut out 1 inch (2.5 cm) circles of
peppermint creams using a plain
cutter. Continue kneading the cut
out scraps and rolling out as before
until all the paste is used. Leave to
dry for 12 hours.

6

Put the chocolate into a bowl,
breaking up the pieces if you are
using block chocolate, and
microwave on HIGH for 4 minutes
or until the chocolate is just
melted. Stir thoroughly.

7

Half-dip the peppermint creams in
the chocolate and place on non-
stick paper until dry.

Makes about 30 pieces.

CHAPTER TWELVE

Jams and Preserves

Making jams, preserves and chutneys in the microwave oven is easy. The colors and flavors are excellent and the process is far less trouble than conventional methods. When using conventional methods it isn't worth making a small quantity of jam or chutney if you have to get out a large preserving pan and scour it afterwards. But with the microwave oven the preserve is made in an ordinary ovenproof glass mixing bowl and sticking is infinitesimal. Microwaved jams and chutneys are completely successful provided you follow the rules for their preparation.

Fruit

Fruit with a high pectin content will be the easiest to cope with so, when first making jam, choose currants, gooseberries, plums or apples. This does not mean that low-pectin fruits such as strawberries are less successful, but it is essential to add lemon juice or commercial pectin to these to help them to set. Jams made from soft fruits thicken on storage, so do not overcook. Either fresh or frozen fruit can be used successfully. See page 100 for instructions on thawing fruit, and remember to include the juices.

Sugar

The fruit must be soft before the sugar is added and the sugar must be well dissolved before the jam is boiled. As a rule the liquid is sufficiently hot after the fruit has been cooked to dissolve the sugar without further cooking at this stage. It helps if you warm the sugar first. To do this put the sugar in its opened bag or in a bowl, preferably lipped, and microwave on HIGH for 3–4 minutes.

Storing

Jams, curds and chutneys should be packed in hot, sterilized jars. Quarter-fill the jars with water and bring to a full boil in the microwave oven. Four jars will take about 1½ minutes, but they will not all come to the boil at the same time. Remove each one as soon as it is ready, using oven gloves, and empty out the water.

For long-term storage use traditional canning jars and lids and then process in a regular hot water bath. For short-term storage you can use freezer-quality plastic wrap and store in the refrigerator.

Fruit curds

Made with eggs and butter as well as fruit and sugar, curds are not a true "preserve" and should only be made in small quantities and eaten quickly. They will keep for up to a month in a cupboard or for up to 3 months in the refrigerator. Lemon curd is particularly easy to make in the microwave oven, and a couple of jars can be made in just a few minutes. Substitute oranges or grapefruit for a change.

Chutneys

The high acid content in chutneys cannot affect an ovenproof glass bowl as it does some metal pans and the mixture is far less likely to burn in the microwave oven than when cooked conventionally as there is no direct contact of heat with the base of the bowl.

The fruits and/or vegetables for a chutney should be finely chopped, sliced or minced. Bruised and poorly shaped ingredients can very often be used as their appearance in the finished preserve is of no account. They are cooked to a pulp with vinegar, sugar, spices and salt. Chutneys do have to be cooked until of a very thick consistency and you must stir frequently during the last minute of cooking. The chutney is ready when no excess liquid remains and the mixture is the consistency of a thick sauce.

Marmalade

With the help of a food processor, marmalade can be made successfully in the microwave oven. Drawing the pectin out of the seeds and pith used to require long, slow cooking. Chopping up the seeds in the food processor overcomes this, making marmalade as quick to cook as jam.

above **Chocolate Truffles (page 116),
Creamy Vanilla Fudge (page 118) and
Coconut Ice (page 119)**

left **Cinnamon Crumble Cake (page 111)
and Frangipane Tart (page 109)**

Blackberry Jam

1¼ cups (225 g) sugar
8 oz (225 g) fresh or frozen
  blackberries, prepared or
  thawed

1

Put the sugar in a 3-quart (2.8-liter) ovenproof glass mixing bowl and microwave on HIGH for 2 minutes or until the sugar is just warm.

2

Add the blackberries, stirring thoroughly.

3

Microwave on HIGH for 3 minutes, stirring every minute to dissolve the sugar (make sure that you stir to the bottom of the bowl). Microwave on HIGH for 5 minutes, by which time the mixture should be boiling rapidly.

4

Stir, then test for setting; 1 tsp (5 ml) of the syrup when dropped on to a chilled plate should wrinkle slightly when pushed with a finger.

5

Put in hot sterilized jars and let cool. Label in the usual way.

Makes about 1 lb (450 g).

Note The jam thickens further as it cools. Do not overcook.

Strawberry Jam Using Frozen Fruit

1 lb (450 g) frozen strawberries
2 Tbsp (30 ml) lemon juice
1 lb (450 g) sugar
pat of butter

1

Thaw the strawberries on LOW for 8–10 minutes. Drain the liquid into a 3-quart (2.8-liter) ovenproof glass mixing bowl and set the strawberries aside.

2

Stir the lemon juice into the strawberry liquid and microwave on HIGH for 2 minutes or until the mixture is boiling.

3

Stir in the sugar and microwave on HIGH for 7 minutes or until the sugar is dissolved. Stir every 2 minutes during cooking.

4

Add the drained strawberries and microwave on HIGH for 5 minutes. Stir in the butter.

5

Microwave on HIGH for 5 minutes, stirring occasionally, and test for setting; 1 tsp (5 ml) jam when dropped on to a chilled plate should wrinkle when pushed with finger. Put in hot sterilized jars and cover and label in the usual way.

Makes 1½ lb (700 g).

Note Do not overcook strawberry jam as it becomes firm on cooling. A weak wrinkle test is generally adequate.

Strawberry Jam Using Fresh Fruit

1 lb (450 g) fresh strawberries, hulled
1 lb (450 g) sugar
2 Tbsp (30 ml) lemon juice

1

Gently mix the strawberries, sugar and lemon juice together in a 3-quart (2.8-liter) ovenproof glass mixing bowl. Cover tightly and leave to stand for 6–8 hours until the strawberries soften and a syrup is formed.

2

Microwave on LOW for 15 minutes or until the sugar is completely dissolved. Stir very gently twice during cooking.

3

Raise the setting and microwave on HIGH for 25 minutes. Test for setting; 1 tsp (5 ml) syrup should wrinkle when dropped on to a chilled plate and pushed with a finger. Put in hot sterilized jars and cover and label in the usual way.

Makes 1½ lb (700 g).

Orange Marmalade

2 lb (900 g) Seville or sweet oranges
2 lemons
2 lb (900 g) sugar
pat of butter

1

Wash and dry the fruit and pare away the thin rind, avoiding the white pith.

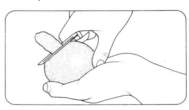

2

Shred or chop the rind, cover and set aside.

3

Chop up the fruit including the pith, flesh and the seeds, which must be broken. A food processor is useful for this.

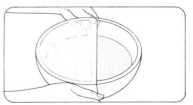

4

Put the chopped mixture into a 3-quart (2.8-liter) ovenproof glass mixing bowl and add 3¾ cups (900 ml) boiling water. Without covering, microwave on HIGH for 15 minutes.

5

Strain the mixture into another large ovenglass bowl and press the cooked pulp until all the juice is squeezed out. Discard the pulp. Stir the shredded rind into the hot juice and microwave on HIGH for 15 minutes or until the rind is tender. Stir twice during cooking. Stir in the sugar until fully dissolved. Half cover the bowl with plastic wrap and microwave on HIGH for 10 minutes.

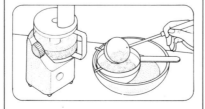

6

Stir in the butter and microwave on HIGH for 5–6 minutes. Stir once during cooking. Test for setting; 1 tsp (5 ml) marmalade should wrinkle when dropped on to a chilled plate. Put in hot sterilized jars and cover and label in the usual way.

Makes 2½ lb (1.1 kg).

Blackcurrant Jam

1 lb (450 g) fresh or frozen
  blackcurrants, prepared or
  thawed
1 lb (450 sugar)

1

Place the blackcurrants in a 3-quart
(2.8-liter) ovenproof glass mixing
bowl. Stir in 2 cups (450 ml) water
and three-quarters cover with
plastic wrap. Microwave on HIGH
for 15 minutes or until the fruit is
very soft, stirring occasionally
during cooking. (Allow an extra 10
minutes if the fruit is frozen.)

2

Put the sugar in another bowl and
microwave on HIGH for 3 minutes
or until the sugar is warm. Add the
sugar to the jam and stir until it
has completely dissolved.

3

Without covering, microwave on
HIGH for 20 minutes or until 1 tsp
(5 ml) of the liquid wrinkles when
dropped on to a chilled plate and
pushed with a fingertip. Stir three
or four times during cooking.

4

Remove from the microwave oven
carefully, using oven gloves. Leave
to cool for 5 minutes then stir
thoroughly. Put in hot sterilized
jars, cover and label.

Makes about 1½ lb (700 g).

Note Do not overcook
blackcurrant jam or it will darken
and develop a caramel flavor. The
jam thickens during cooling.

Lemon Curd

4 large lemons
4 eggs, beaten
1¼ cups (225 g) granulated sugar
½ cup (125 g) unsalted butter

1

Finely grate the rind from the
lemons and place in a 3-quart (2.8-
liter) ovenproof glass mixing bowl.
Squeeze the juice from the lemons
and add to the beaten eggs. Strain
into the bowl.

2

Stir in the sugar, then add the
butter, cut into 4 or 6 pieces.
Microwave on HIGH for 1 minute,
stir, then microwave for 5 minutes
or until the lemon curd is thick.
Whisk well every minute (this is
important to avoid curdling).

3

When the lemon curd is thick,
remove the bowl from the
microwave oven using oven gloves
and continue whisking until the
mixture is cool. Lemon curd
thickens on cooling.

4

Put in hot sterilized jars, cover,
label and store in the refrigerator.

Makes 2 lb (900 g).

Note Lemon curd will keep for
about 1 month, after which it
begins to deteriorate.

Tomato Chutney

1½ lb (700 g) firm, greenish-red
  tomatoes
8 oz (225 g) cooking apples,
  peeled and cored
1 medium onion, peeled
⅔ cup (125 g) dark brown sugar
1 cup (125 g) raisins
1 level tsp (5 ml) salt
1 cup (200 ml) cider vinegar
½ oz (15 g) ground ginger
¼ level tsp (1.25 ml) cayenne
  pepper
½ level tsp (2.5 ml) dry mustard

1

Put the tomatoes in a 3-quart
(2.8-liter) ovenproof glass bowl
and just cover with boiling water.
Microwave on HIGH for 4 minutes,
then lift out the tomatoes one by
one using a slotted spoon or fork
and remove the skins.

2

Mince the apple and onion or chop
finely in the food processor to a
thick paste. Roughly chop the
tomatoes.

3

Mix all the chutney ingredients
together in a 3-quart (2.8-liter)
ovenproof glass mixing bowl.
Three-quarters cover with plastic
wrap and microwave on HIGH for
45 minutes or until the mixture is
thick and all the liquid absorbed.
Stir every 5 minutes during
cooking and take particular care,
stirring more frequently, during
the last 5 minutes.

4

Leave to stand for 10 minutes, then
stir, pour into hot sterilized jars,
cover and label. Store for at least 2
months before using.

Makes 2 lb (900 g).

Index